reworking
success
new communities
at the millennium

reworking
success
new communities
at the millennium

robert theobald

NEW SOCIETY PUBLISHERS

Canadian Cataloguing in Publication Data:

Theobald, Robert
 Reworking Success

Includes bibliographical references.
ISBN 0-86571-366-9 (bound) -- ISBN 0-86571-367-7 (pbk.)

 1. Community. 2. Social ecology. 3. Human ecology. 4.
Social change. 5. Forecasting. I. Title
HT166.T53 1997   307   C97-910094-1

A catalog record for this publication is available from the National
Library of Canada and the Library of Congress.

Cover design by Miriam MacPhail.

Printed in Canada on acid-free, partially recycled (20 percent post-
consumer) paper using soy-based inks by Best Book Manufacturers.

Inquiries regarding requests to reprint all or part of *Reworking Success*
should be addressed to New Society Publishers at the address below.
Paperback ISBN: 0-86571-367-7
Hardback ISBN: 0-86571-366-9

To order directly from the publishers, please add $3.00 to the price of
the first copy, and $1.00 for each additional copy (plus GST in Canada).
Send check or money order to:

New Society Publishers
P.O. Box 189, Gabriola Island, BC Canada V0R 1X0

New Society Publishers aims to publish books for fundamental social
change through nonviolent action. We focus especially on sustainable
living, progressive leadership, and educational and parenting
resources. Our full list of books can be browsed on the World Wide Web
at: http://www.newsociety.com

NEW SOCIETY PUBLISHERS
Gabriola Island BC, Canada and Stony Creek CT, U.S.A.

table of contents

acknowledgments

These lectures were improved by significant feedback from many people using the Internet. There are, unfortunately, far too many of them to credit individually. This material also reflects innumerable conversations and much reading over my forty-year working life. The successes belong to all of us; the errors and weaknesses are my own.

Reworking Success was originally written to be broadcast throughout Canada for a prestigious annual lecture series. However, the lectures were cancelled at the eleventh hour.

The process of developing the lectures was unusual in that the author, Robert Theobald, chose to place the texts on the Internet for public feedback and input. We learned of the texts through a member of our local economics discussion group which meets every two weeks. He had downloaded them, thinking that they would make appropriate subject matter for consideration by the group, and encouraged members to attend a public lecture by Theobald in the neighboring town.

New Society Publishers later made contact with Robert Theobald, and decided to publish *Reworking Success* in book form. Our decision was based on believing that Theobald makes an important statement on the human predicament as we reach the turn of the century, and that the audience he originally intended to reach through the lectures should have wide public access to his ideas. In addition, Theobald urges citizens to act to help create fundamental social change — a unique and refreshing feature that we feel is especially appropriate in these times, and particularly suited to a publisher committed to bringing to public attention works that promote such fundamental change.

By originally placing his texts on the Internet for public input and debate, Robert Theobald was demonstrating unusual faith in the democratic and participatory process that he himself advocates. After cancellation of the lectures, Theobald has continued to seek public engagement in his ideas, and to use the texts as a catalyst for real change at the community level.

It is in this same spirit of open and democratic engagement that we now publish *Reworking Success*, and urge you to join in whatever ways you can in the discussion of humanity's future and action for effective change.

Christopher Plant
New Society Publishers

A stranger comes to a starving town,
Promising to make stone soup.

He finds some firewood,
Uses his own pot,
Puts water on to boil.

As the water heats,
He wanders around,
Selecting,
Rejecting,
Cleaning
Stones.

He adds them to the pot,
Carefully,
With strange muttered recipes.

Intrigued,
The villagers gather round.
This is the best entertainment
Their village has had since the famine began.

As they listen,
They hear the stranger admit
That while stone soup is good,
It does taste better with a pinch of salt.

One of the crazier people,
(Or is she actually more caring?)
Brings out some salt she has hoarded.

The stranger
Gets bolder,
Suggests carrots,
And potatoes,
And swedes,
And dried tomatoes
And herbs.
As each one is added,
Others remember their own stores
And bring them to the common stew.

We have all made something out of nothing,
By remembering the old, old lesson,
That together we can create opportunities
Which escape us when we hide
Our resources and skills from others.

It is time to build community again,
To share what we have,
And to experience miracles.

It is time to live,
Expecting grace
And finding it,
Daily,
Even hourly,
In the midst
Of our harried lives.

Robert Theobald

M ost of us are familiar with the cliché, "You can't argue with success." After all, when one accomplishes one's goals, breaks a world record, or publishes a best-selling book, what is there to argue about? Success, however, can be a personal burden. We all know stories about outstanding athletes who achieve Olympic gold at the age of 17; life then risks becoming a downhill grade with everything that comes later seeming a pale shadow of that early accomplishment. The penalties of success can also be felt secondhand, as sometimes happens when children live in the shadow of their parents' fame and success.

Success can also be a collective burden when it changes the conditions in which we live and alters the goals we aim to achieve. While all organisms inevitably strive for success, human beings alone have the capacity to change their surroundings so dramatically and rapidly that they must alter their patterns of behavior, reward systems, and, ultimately, their success criteria. When this happens, new cultural patterns must emerge if severe breakdowns are to be avoided.

Fortunately, we now know the directions in which we must move: the required success criteria for the twenty-first century are ecological integrity, effective decision-making, and social cohesion. These are progressively replacing current commitments to maximum economic growth, compulsive consumption, and international competition.

This change in success criteria will necessarily occur at the personal, group, and community level rather than through top-down policy shifts. A primary way in which people can personally grasp the meaning of this change is through rethinking their attitudes to work and the distribution of resources.

I have aimed to summarize my position in my title.

"Reworking Success" argues that we can no longer continue in current directions; my subtitle, "New Communities at the Millennium," stresses the need for action at the local level.

Core questions

There are a number of key questions which determine the way one looks at the future. I summarize them here:

a) What is the time-scale for change? I have assumed a fifteen year period in which dramatic changes will be completed, with much having taken place by the end of the millennium.

b) What is the world's carrying capacity? There are estimates ranging from one billion people to 10 billion; it is extremely unlikely that the world's population will stabilize below 10 billion unless there are massive catastrophes. I am convinced that the viable level of production and waste for such a population is way below that of current rich countries. Fortunately, a higher quality of life can be achieved using far fewer resources.

c) At what scale should decisions be made? Some decisions are moving from the nation-state to more local levels, some are moving to the multinational and the global. How are decisions made about appropriate scales for decision-making? I am convinced that only broad, tough, citizen participation can solve our problems.

d) What forms of politics (collective decision-making) are appropriate for the twenty-first century? The proposals being made range from the redevelopment of a highly elitist system to far deeper citizen involvement. My belief is that we must move toward the latter.

e) Are people defined by "original sin" or "original blessing?" The assumption which lies behind this work is that most people, most of the time, want to develop themselves and help other people develop. I cannot imagine a viable future if this is not true.

Different responses

There seem to be three different levels of reaction to my proposal for fundamentally changed directions. One group of people is all too aware of the challenges that humanity faces. They are therefore sympathetic to the arguments presented and delighted that these ideas are being advanced. While there is considerable disagreement within this group, those within it share a common belief that new positive directions can be achieved through the thought and action of committed citizens. There is also agreement that we shall only make progress as we change from concentrating on problems to becoming excited about opportunities. The emphasis on working together in new ways — expressed in Chapters 4 and 5 — and the scenario material in Chapter 7 may contain the most new material for this group. Their primary use of the material, however, may be through sharing it with others with whom they are working.

The second group is composed of those forward-looking thinkers who work in business and education, labor and politics, social services and finance, law and health, nonprofits, planning, and many other fields. These people are recognizing that their traditional answers and policy measures are no longer effective. They are looking for new directions although they are not sure they dare announce publicly the development of their thinking. There is a sharp contrast between committee and boardroom discussions and the material which is given out to the media. A recent trip through Canada confirmed for me that there are people in all organizations who would be willing to lead in new directions but feel constrained by their position. People in this group will find that the material in their field is limited, and perhaps even simplistic, but that ideas about other areas will, I hope, be illuminating.

The third group will find the material and analyses novel, and perhaps even somewhat threatening. Those who are in this category and who still choose to follow my argument to its conclusion, might see themselves as acquiring new factual information and also having a chance to test their current thinking against a significantly different perspective. In order to do this, however, they must be willing not only to look at questions in new ways, but also to work with a significantly different style compared to most academic texts.

Complexity overload

As I look around me I see a large number of people who find life so complex and overloaded that they are no longer participating in community life. The reactions of those who are still committed to achieving change seem to vary with age.

People in their fifties, sixties, and seventies, like myself, are constantly surprised by the differences between the world in which they grew up and the norms which now exist. It almost seems as though a buzzer goes off several times a day as individuals are struck by the dissonances between the past and the present.

Those still at school or university are often frustrated because they are being taught about the structure and functioning of a world which has already vanished — a world they never knew and never will know. The most committed members of this generation want to have a voice in the ongoing dialogue, with their opinions being seriously considered in the decision-making process.

Most of those in their twenties through fifties are so occupied in meeting the challenges posed by their work and family obligations that they feel they can put aside little time for their community and society. The decrease in the time available from this group preoccupies voluntary agencies around the world.

When people question me about my work, they often seem to assume that the audience for general lectures and seminars given by those engaged in futurist activities would be in the 18-40 range. In fact, my colleagues tell me that their audience composition is usually similar to my own — a few dubious young people, a small number of people in their thirties and forties who often seem preoccupied with other matters, while the bulk of the audience consists of those in their fifties to seventies, anxious, somewhat uncomfortable, and actively seeking answers.

We need to involve all age groups in the co-creation of new goals for the twenty-first century, particularly the young because they both bring new perspectives and have the most at stake. I hope that this material may play a small part in this effort. The basic goal is to create an opening for all of us to seize the opportunities which exist so abundantly at this time.

September 1996
New Orleans, and Dingwall

part 1

successes become failures

the burden of success

L ooking back over the most recent Massey Lectures is a sobering experience. One message dominates, expressed in a number of very different voices and styles. Societies everywhere, we're told, are failing to cope with the challenges of our times. The possibility of political and financial collapse is very real, because our institutions are obsessed with economic issues rather than dealing with social, cultural, and environmental challenges. A few sentences from three of the recent Massey Lectures will give you a sense of the overall message.

Ursula Franklin said in 1990, "It is my conviction that nothing short of a global reformulation of major social forces and of the social contract can end this historical period of profound and violent transformations, and give a manner of security to the world and its citizens. Such a development will require the redefinition of rights and responsibilities, and the setting of limits to power and control."

Conor Cruise O'Brien said in 1994, "It seems to me that an alarmingly high proportion of communicators, on the eve of the millennium, are suffering from some sort of cognitive degeneration. . . . The picture of the world that we are receiving is a curious mixture of fact and fiction. The facts, very often in the form of pictures, are very often horrifying. The fiction comes into the commentary and interpretation, heavily charged with wishful fantasy, unwarranted reassurances, and intimations of quick fixes."

And in his 1995 lectures, John Ralston Saul said, "There is a general sense that our civilization is in a long-term crisis. It can be seen from its political or social or economic aspect. From each angle, the same crisis can be seen differently. . . we have drifted further out into a cold, unfriendly, confusing sea. The new certitude of those in positions of authority — those out of the water — is that the certain answer is to cut away the life preservers."

On the other hand, this past spring, broadcast journalist Gwynne Dyer put forward a very different view in his CBC radio series called "Millennium." Dyer argued that we were moving inexorably into far better times. He said, "I think that in the end the principles of equality and individualism will produce democratic societies almost everywhere, and much more humane societies at that."

I share both the hopes and the fears. Tom Atlee, a close colleague and author who has coined the term "co-intelligence," catches current realities in his statement, "Things are getting better and better and worse and worse faster and faster." Those who are bleakly pessimistic about the future deny the proven capacity of human beings to be creative in their own communities. That's why I'm hopeful. I also believe Gwynne Dyer is far too optimistic because, as a rational analyst, I know the difficulties of making fundamental changes. Current systems have enormous inertia. We live inside them, and so we continue to act in old-fashioned ways we think will ensure short-run survival. They won't.

There is one certainty at the current time. There will be huge changes in the next decades. George Land caught the issue with his book title *Breakpoint and Beyond*. As you will discover, I believe that the probable future is negative. But there is no reason we have to accept this result. We can co-create a more positive future.

Old issues, new responses

My experience shows that people are ready for new opportunities. Think about how avalanches start: when conditions are ripe, the immediate cause can be very minor. The same is true for cultural shifts. The real challenge today is to learn how to act as though what we do can make a difference. As the anthropologist Margaret Mead said, "Never doubt that a small group of committed people can change the world. Indeed it is the only thing which ever has."

The issues we face have been defined for decades and people have been coming to grips with them over this time period. Thirty-two years ago, in 1964, a small group of people from very different walks of life and with very different life-histories sent a report to the then-president of the United States, Lyndon Johnson, that set out the nature of the challenge. The language still sounds remarkably up to date. We called our report *The Triple Revolution* and in it we talked about cybernation — a word used at that time to describe the combined impact of computers and robots. Here's what we said:

"Cybernation is manifesting the characteristics of a revolution in production. These include the development of radically different techniques and the subsequent appearance of novel principles of the organization of production, a basic reordering of man's relationship to his environment, and a dramatic increase in total available and potential energy.

"The major difference between the agricultural, industrial, and cybernation revolutions is the speed at which they developed. The agricultural revolution began several thousand years ago in the Middle East. Centuries passed in the shift from a subsistence base of hunting and gathering to settled agriculture.

"In contrast, it has been less than 200 years since the emergence of the industrial revolution, and direct and accurate knowledge of the new productive techniques has reached most of mankind. . . .

"The fundamental problem posed by the cybernation revolution is that it invalidates the general mechanism so far used to undergird people's rights as consumers. Up to this time economic resources have been distributed on the basis of contributions to production, with machines and men competing for employment on somewhat equal terms. In the developing cybernated system, potentially unlimited output can be achieved by systems of machines which will require little cooperation from human beings. As machines take over production from men, they absorb an increasing proportion of resources while the men who are displaced become dependent on minimal and unrelated government measures — unemployment insurance, social security, and welfare payments.

"These measures are less and less able to disguise a historic paradox: that a substantial proportion of the population is subsisting on minimum incomes, often below the poverty line, at a time when sufficient productive potential is available to supply the needs of everyone."

I have quoted from this 1964 report at length for two reasons. First, I think it is important to realize that today's developing crises were visible at least thirty years ago, and the negative consequences we see around us could therefore have been palliated. Second, it leads me into a primary topic of these lectures. I want to examine the failure of our societies to provide opportunity and income on the one hand, and social services on the other, to an ever-growing number of people. The situation is worse in the United States and many of the poor countries than in Canada and Europe, but government cutbacks clearly threaten the safety nets in these nations as well.

A great many people in government do not seem to make the connection between the budget cuts they administer and the consequences "on the ground." The reduced services, which seem separate in accounting terms, actually affect individuals, families, and whole communities in ways which compound exponentially.

This problem is no secret. Economic inequality and rising unemployment have been front-page news lately. An extraordinary series of articles in the Canadian newspaper, *The Globe and Mail*, in the Spring of 1996 challenged many current myths. The most remarkable piece, to my mind, was one which showed the different experiences of three generations in one family. The parents had a radically easier time than the grandparents. But the children, who were mainly in their twenties, were once again struggling as their grandparents had. They saw their prospects getting worse, not better.

Worries exist throughout the developed world: there has been a brief period of euphoric prosperity which has already ended. The picture is equally bleak as one examines the experiences of the developing areas of the world. United Nations figures show that in 70 countries, citizens are on average poorer than they were in 1980. In 43 countries, they are poorer than they were in 1970.

According to Victor Keegan, a political affairs commentator

writing in the British newspaper, *The Guardian*, the richest 20 per cent of the world's population increased their share of total global wealth from 70 per cent to 85 per cent over the same period, while the poorest lost ground moving down from 2.3 per cent to 1.4 per cent. The wealth of Bill Gates, founder of Microsoft Corporation (the world's premier software company), and the richest man in the world with $20 billion in U.S. funds, is greater by itself than that of half a dozen poor countries, according to Keegan.

I want to look further at our failure to use knowledge three decades ago. If we knew so much back then, an awkward question emerges. What have I, and all of us, been doing for the past three decades? Why are we still going over ground which we had defined quite well so long ago, again and again and again? How have we failed to realize the dangers which will inevitably emerge as jobs are taken over by computers and the employment which remains becomes less well-paid?

Here's one clue. At the end of the 1960s, I was employed by the United Nations to visit the heads of their organizations and to discuss the future. I talked to several people in the International Labor Organization, whose responsibility it was to deal with employment policy. I argued that, given emerging technological developments, full employment could not be achieved. They did not argue whether I was right or not — they simply maintained that it "had" to be possible because their mandate demanded that this approach be maintained.

Despite the now overwhelming evidence, governments still remain unwilling to face the implications of rising unemployment and inequality for work patterns and the way we distribute resources. Indeed, this is just one area in which we refuse to look at the urgent issues now confronting us. I hope in these lectures to open up this taboo issue, as well as others, so we can discuss them creatively.

Real change happens

The public agenda can be changed on the basis of a well placed effort and a healthy dose of luck. The reason I am convinced that ideas can bring about real change emerges from one of my critical life-experiences which I have already mentioned: the publication of *The Triple Revolution.*

The attention paid to it was a fluke: we got front-page coverage in *The New York Times.* Among other things, *The Triple Revolution* proposed Basic Economic Security for all — one version of the guaranteed annual income, a national program which would have provided everybody with minimal resources. This idea seemed outrageous to many editorial writers, but their attack on this one aspect drew attention to the central thesis of the document: that computers and robots, modern weaponry, and the drive toward human rights would inevitably change the world in ways which would surprise us all. The proposal for Basic Economic Security was vigorously argued in Canada as well as in the United States and Europe.

The process by which The *Triple Revolution* was created taught me many lessons and, as I'll be doing throughout these lectures, I'll use my own experience to illustrate more general points. A group of us had been exchanging drafts of *The Triple Revolution* for a long time. Just before Christmas 1963, a new draft came in. Disgusted with our failure to make any significant progress, I tossed it into the wastebasket. My anthropologist and historian colleague, Jeanne-Marie Scott, pulled it out, forced me to work on it with her, and together we discovered the wordings that made the document newsworthy.

The Triple Revolution was successful because of several factors simultaneously aligning at the same point, producing a "cusp." It was the right document at the right time in the right style. Is there a similar cusp point at this moment in history? I believe there is. I think people are more and more dismayed by the direction in which our societies are moving and are hungry for opportunities to think and work with each other to achieve new directions. I think they are tired of the divisions between left and right, management and labor, young and old, men and women, and want to start working with each other across current boundaries.

Creative choices

Jacques Ellul's 1964 book, *La Technique* (*The Technological Society*), is a good place to start looking for an understanding of what has gone wrong. He showed us how economics and technology force us to search for "the one best way." Ellul perceived how this drive, if it were permitted to continue, would destroy the spontaneity of life and our ability to make choices. This danger is visible every time a politician, businessman, or academic announces that we "must" move in a particular direction because there are "no choices."

We all have our own horror stories about the assumed compulsion toward efficiency regardless of its impact on people, communities, or the environment. Mine centre on the chief executive officers and top managers who announce they "have no choice" but to fire hundreds, or thousands, of workers. Why is there so little effective resistance to the idea that firing workers is the way to increase profits, I wonder? And my anger increases when I discover that the CEOs feel they "have no choice" but to increase dramatically their own salaries at the same time.

A recent poll in the United States showed that I am not alone in these feelings. Large majorities see corporate behavior as a "serious national problem." When asked if reduced benefits (health care and pensions) are a "serious problem" or not, 82 per cent say yes. Large layoffs during times of profitability are regarded as a "serious problem" by 81 per cent; huge CEO salaries (which are now 225 times as large as the average worker's pay) are a "serious problem" for 79 per cent, and stagnant wages (wages that don't keep up with the rising cost of living) are a "serious problem" for 76 per cent.

People do not buy the explanation that recent corporate behavior is required by a competitive global economy. Only 22 per cent of those surveyed said they thought competition motivated corporate behavior; 70 per cent said they thought greed was the motivating factor (seven per cent said they didn't know). This view — that greed is what motivates corporations, not competition — crosses all age groups, all races, all educational backgrounds, and all incomes. It even crosses political parties: 79 per cent of Democrats, and 63 per cent of Republicans said they thought corporate greed explains downsizing, stagnant wages, and reduced job benefits.

The "no choice" rhetoric is no longer acceptable to more and more people. This is, of course, just as well, for if we accept that there are "no choices," thinking inevitably stops. There is little point in dialogue if the outcome is preordained and unchangeable. A primary challenge today is to show that the existing dominant viewpoint is not the only way to view the world — that there are several possible approaches to our moment in history.

Getting away from the idea that economics and technology override everything else is not going to be easy. After all, it's not easy to change any conventional view. When somebody warns, "Look out: those ideas and attitudes you've held so long and so firmly are not good for you," the common reaction is to retreat into a psychic bunker and deny responsibility. All too many of us decide that there's nothing useful we can do about the enormous problems that loom over us, ignoring the evidence that the actions of individuals and groups have made a difference in the past and can continue to do so into the future.

In 1897 the French sociologist Emile Durkheim coined the term "anomie" to describe the psychological problems he observed in many individuals. Literally meaning "without a name," anomie described the state of a person who was "normless," who could not find a role in the society that had grown up around him. Jeanne-Marie Scott felt the problem today was different and therefore coined another word, "amondie," meaning "without a world," which described the rather general feeling that events no longer make sense, and that the world they once inhabited has apparently disappeared.

I often take a poll at the beginning of my lectures. My last questions are: "Do you read science fiction?" "Do you not read science fiction?" "Do you know if you read science fiction?" The last question always gets a laugh. I go on to say that my minimal goal is for people to recognize just how bizarre many of the stories they read every day are.

The conditions in which we currently live have been created because we have failed to challenge so-called economic and technological imperatives. These are driving us toward efficiency and away from a common recognition of our complex and diverse humanity and the globe's fragility. If we are to develop a higher quality of life, the first step is to recognize that there are many ways to deal with all issues.

It is not true that we must continually crank up the economic machine, starve the poor, and work ourselves to death. Believe me about this: I was trained as an economist! The challenge is to set imagination and creativity loose, to think outside the box, to see the opportunities which lie beyond the problems. We can only resolve today's questions by opening up new approaches and seeing new connections. Fortunately a broad and general move away from obsessive problem-solving and toward a search for new opportunities is already underway.

Here's a current example. It seems that the issue of abortion hopelessly divides public opinion. And yet there is a way of restating the issue. Angry activists who have come together in some communities in the United States have found that one thing they all want is to decrease the number of unwelcome pregnancies. Rethinking the abortion issue also leads to an agreement on the need for better contraceptive techniques. If it's true that as many as 50 per cent of births are still unplanned, surely it's time that we made contraceptive development one of our highest research priorities. Recognition of the potential of this kind of common ground on a wider scale would bring about a new kind of political dialogue.

This is one example of the work of common ground advocates, who search for ways to bring opponents together. This approach, which is fortunately gathering force around the world, assumes that we all have part of the truth. I recognized this reality clearly when I was asked to speak at a convention of Methodist religious educators. They'd looked back at their history and found out I was a speaker at their first meeting and now they wanted me to come to their twentieth. I saw the invitation as a chance to see how people would react to my changed thinking. After my speech, I waited around to find out what issues people might want to raise with me. An older woman came up and said, "I really appreciated your message today, it was very meaningful." I thanked her. She went on, "You really were an arrogant man when you talked to us twenty years ago."

She was right. Twenty years before, which was at the end of the sixties, I was reasonably sure I knew where the culture needed to go. Today, I think I can define some of the questions we must address if we are to take advantage of the extraordinary possibilities which now exist. I am certain, however, that neither

I nor anybody else knows enough to prescribe directions. We need to listen and learn from each other if we are to avoid following the historical pattern which condemns us to cultural collapse.

The historical pattern is clear: cultures rise and fall. They fail to change their success criteria as conditions alter around them; they therefore decline and new societies take their place. Success has burdened cultures many times in the past. The collapses have sometimes been ecological. Successful cultures have seen their populations grow. This growth has stressed the capacity of the local ecosystems to provide food, and eventually bad weather or bad planning destroyed previously flourishing cultures. This pattern is clearly visible in the anthropological record. Much of the Middle East was ravaged in earlier millennia by over-grazing and overuse of soils: green and pleasant lands became deserts.

Cultures throughout history have also collapsed when citizens were unable to find roles within a changing socioeconomy, while others benefited and enjoyed increased affluence. At the peak of the Roman Empire, it was government policy that Italian Romans should remain in the homeland, supported by food and other supplies from a huge empire which was defended against the so-called barbarians by troops recruited from within the conquered territories. The isolated, purposeless, well-fed inhabitants of Rome were entertained by increasingly bizarre and violent exhibitions in the arenas. Roman society was dominated by the provision of "bread and circuses." Citizenship declined, leadership failed, social structures broke down, and eventually the empire was overwhelmed by more organized and energetic external enemies.

Our challenge is to avoid this recurrent pattern, which we can now see developing in our own times. There are two primary reasons. First, the collapse of cultures is not pleasant for those who live within them. Second, we now live within a global culture and if industrial era patterns break down, they will have profoundly destructive consequences throughout the world and not just in a specific area or nation, as has been the case in the past.

Measuring success

At one level, our challenge is not new. Humanity has moved from hunting and gathering to agriculture, from agriculture to industry, and is now moving out of the industrial era into a profoundly new set of conditions. There are two critical differences, however. First, there's the very fact that we all live within a global culture. Second, there's the ever-increasing speed of change and the consequent obsolescence of the ways we measure change in our societies.

The most critical evidence that industrial-era success, as defined in industrial-era terms, is damaging our future can be seen by comparing old and emerging statistical measures. The primary mechanism currently used around the world to determine how well societies are doing is the measure called the Gross Domestic Product (GDP). The GDP is calculated by adding the combined production of agriculture, mining, industry, and services. It was originally designed when production of goods was all-important and has only been partially updated to deal with the current emergence of services in worldwide markets. It is important to stress that the original purpose of calculating the GDP was purely economic: it was never meant to measure the success of societies in the way it is, unfortunately, often used today.

Analysts agree that there are many problems with the GDP. For example, it counts "bads," such as reconstruction following a natural disaster and expenses to protect from crime, as well as "goods," such as the building of housing and schools. When I was in Nebraska in the middle of a deep recession, I stated that the best way to improve the prospects for the state, given conventional measures, was for the State Capitol to burn down. Nonsensical statements of this type are now taken for granted: it is conventionally argued that economic disasters such as hurricanes and earthquakes are good for the economy. Another problem with the GDP is that it does not take account of resource depletion or pollution. Nor does it include the value of unpaid housework or repairs. A new indicator has therefore been developed in the United States called the Genuine Progress Indicator (GPI) which corrects many of the GDP problems and creates a more relevant measure of success and failure. In

Canada, the government agency Statistics Canada has replicated this approach. While the GDP has been increasing annually, the United States GPI reveals a decline of one per cent a year in the seventies, two per cent a year in the eighties, and six per cent a year in the early nineties. Similar calculation in Canada shows that the GPI is currently more or less stable.

If we are to be able to bring about the required fundamental changes in a relevant time-frame, we shall require an effective and widely-shared communications system. Unfortunately, our success in creating huge volumes of information is burdening our decision-making systems with so much data that they are less and less effective. The flood of information, and the growing opportunity to personalize it, does, of course, provide extraordinary potentials. For example, each individual's total medical history can now be on a credit-card-sized "smart card." In case of sudden illness or accident, all vital information could be accessed immediately. The gains are clear, but there are equally obvious possibilities for misuse in a world where more and more decisions are made primarily to minimize medical costs rather than to provide high-quality care. At the other end of the information spectrum from our high-tech "smart cards," the complete lack of access to even elementary computer technologies for most of those currently disadvantaged is making routes out of poverty difficult to find. Those who cannot work with electronic information will be left further and further behind.

The drive to produce

Given these enormous shifts in the ways we currently live, it is extraordinary that we continue to believe that the ideas advanced by Adam Smith in the late eighteenth century are still valid. When Adam Smith, "father of the industrial revolution," wrote his book, The Wealth of Nations, he certainly did not envisage such a crowded and environmentally-distressed world. Nor did he anticipate consumption would become the driving force behind modern economies.

Adam Smith started the drive toward rationalization of production — the process by which maximum production is achieved with minimum inputs of labor, capital, and land. His views sound strangely modern. He showed how the production of pins was increased if each worker performed one task rather than manufacturing the whole pin. He talked about ten workers turning out more than 48,000 pins in a day rather than the maximum of 100 which could be crafted if each individual worked on the whole process by themselves. Industry continues to increase production in this way by mechanizing work and dividing it into smaller and smaller pieces. Every day we hear about the growing capacities of modern machinery which will continue to make employees less and less necessary.

The world's confidence in economic growth assisted by technology results, however, from faulty thinking. From Adam Smith on, economists have convinced almost everybody that our goal must be to increase production. If only we can increase the availability of goods and services, they argue, social problems will eventually be resolved and success will be assured. In fact, increased production has always been inevitable, given the way the capitalist economy is organized. The capacity to produce has therefore risen fairly steadily since the 1820s. There have been peaks and valleys of over-and under-production caused partly by variations in what Austrian economist, Joseph Schumpeter, writing in the early twentieth century, called the "animal spirits" of entrepreneurs. Production, nevertheless, has continued to move ever upwards.

Economist Robert Heilbroner demonstrated in his 1992 book, *Twenty-first Century Capitalism*, that this sustained growth in production, and the consequent social tragedies, are both core realities of the capitalist system. Heilbroner also showed that the introduction of capitalism forces profound shifts in social and cultural norms. Throughout the nineteenth century, achieving the desired increase in production was hampered by the unreliable habits of workers. As soon as they had earned enough money for their immediate needs, they would leave their jobs. Indeed, their primary goal was often to earn enough to afford a drunken binge. This frustrated employers: they increasingly wanted year-round workers who would meet deadlines. It was therefore vital that workers learn to perceive jobs as desirable in themselves, evidence of their skill and strength. Casey, the steel-driving man of the railroad songs of a hundred years ago, illustrated how successful this manipulation was. Jobs gradually became the centre of life for more and more people.

Jobs were not only made to seem necessary for self-esteem, they also became increasingly rewarding financially. In the nineteenth century, most workers were ill-paid by modern standards. A massive shift occurred when Henry Ford decided, in the early twentieth century, that the only way to enable enough people to buy his mass-produced automobiles was to pay employees the then extraordinarily high wage of five dollars per day. Ford, the pioneer of mass production, revealed that the real problem in economic systems was not determining how to produce more efficiently, but finding ways to sell what could be produced.

Henry Ford's decision to make money available to workers so that they could be consumers became the industrial model that kept the economy moving forward through the twenties. There was, however, an unanticipated consequence of this emphasis on consumption: people came to believe in endless prosperity. They therefore invested heavily in the stock market, buying on margin — that is, on borrowed money. When the stockmarket eventually crashed in 1929, a Great Depression followed. As the thirties progressed, a debate developed about which policies and strategies could cope most effectively with the Depression. The conventional wisdom was that supply and demand should, and would, eventually come into balance, and the less the government interfered, the more rapidly conditions would right themselves. This viewpoint became less and less credible as the decade progressed.

Then came the landmark book by John Maynard Keynes, under the title of *The General Theory of Employment, Interest, and Money*. In retrospect his argument seems obvious: Keynes said it was possible for demand to stagnate below potential supply. But even though he explained what was actually going on when others had been unable to do so, most economists rejected his arguments because they seemed too novel to be credible. As a result of the storm of criticism, Keynes' theories initially received scant political attention and did little to change public policy in the 1930s.

The slump ended with the onset of World War II. The necessity for maximum wartime production meant that industrial capacity became the bottleneck for the first time in a decade and remained a constraint through the 1970s. In the 1980s we once again moved back to a production glut.

The economic glider

A new image may help us to grasp the ways we shall need to behave in the future. Herman Daly, an economist who challenges the growth ethic, has suggested that our present economic system is like a jet plane that must fly at high speed, because otherwise it will stall and crash. He suggested that we should start to think about a helicopter which could hover. A helicopter, however, is both fuel-inefficient and noisy. I propose that we start thinking about a glider as our symbol for the future.

I recognize the danger of pushing any analogy too far, but there are some fascinating thoughts which emerge as one considers the operation of a glider. First, any activity will inevitably use up resources at its beginning. The appropriate questions are: first, what is the minimum effective amount of resources needed to accomplish the purpose; second, will the gain compensate for the expenditure of energy? Following on from that, we can see that just as an experienced pilot can find a thermal when the less skilled may miss it, an individual who knows how to carry through an activity has a far greater chance of succeeding than the uninformed.

Consider how brilliantly the glider is designed for its purpose. The post-industrial world will not have the resources to tolerate the over-design and waste which is so common today. Overcoming problems by brute force, rather than by using imagination and knowledge, will not be acceptable in the future.

Finally, the image of the glider reminds us that nothing lasts forever: the craft eventually comes back to earth regardless of the skill of the pilot. We urgently need to relearn that just as we are afraid of personal death, we are also profoundly unwilling to recognize that institutions can long outlive their usefulness. Huge amounts of waste are tolerated as we prop up obsolete profit, nonprofit, and governmental institutions. People work in situations where their energy is badly used instead of moving on to new situations where they can contribute.

Current socioeconomic strategies stress human, computer, and technological systems to the maximum. The goal is to work at 100 per cent of capacity and possibly above! When crises come, there is little energy to cope with potentially disastrous consequences. Look, for example, at the air traffic control system. Air controllers are asked to do more than is humanly feasible. The human costs are very high. In addition, the risk of accidents is increased. This is a recipe for disaster.

The alternative is to design human systems with "surplus capacity" so we work within the reasonable limits of human attention. In a few areas we have recognized this need for the surplus capacity, recognizing that systems have to be down some of the time. We do not expect firefighters to fight fires continuously: our measurement of their effectiveness is in terms of response time in crises. In this case, society recognizes that efficiency and ability does decline beyond a certain point.

This type of thinking can now be applied throughout more and more of society. People need the opportunity to be in peak form rather than be measured simply by the number of hours they work. Continuing toil and overload makes little sense when computers, and machines controlled by them, can take over more and more repetitive activity. People can move back to more comfortable rhythms. And there is lots of evidence that they want to do so. But in order to take this step successfully we shall have to change our socioeconomic structures so that people can be ensured both meaningful work and access to resources.

the citizen as euphoric consumer: 1945-1973

There have been two distinct periods since the end of World War II. The first created Grand Expectations, to borrow the title of James Patterson's book. This was the period up to the resignation of the president of the United States, Richard Nixon. It was a time when economic and social trends seemed to be moving in very positive directions. The second period, from the mid-seventies until today, has been very different. While horizons seemed wide open at the end of the sixties, prospects narrowed with the oil embargoes. Intellectual thinking also shifted dramatically, with a split between deep Malthusian pessimism and highly optimistic economic and technological determinism.

It is difficult to get a firm grasp on our moment in history because these two startlingly different periods, before and after the mid-seventies, are interpreted in radically different ways by various people. Even now, many continue to hope that the patterns of success achieved in the first thirty years after World War II can continue into the future. Others argue, as I do, that these decades were a unique period that can never be repeated. The ideas which were established then cannot reasonably be seen as a model for the future.

Economic unrealities

When I decided to study economics at Cambridge University in the late forties I never guessed that the subject would come to dominate society in the way it has over the last fifty years. I learned a discipline based on nineteenth-century physical science which assumed objective, quantifiable, cause-and-effect relationships. We are still largely using these past patterns of thought despite the growing understanding of chaos and complexity theories which deny their validity.

We were taught two sets of theories. In what's known as neoclassical economics, all businesses were presumed to be small, there were no labor unions, no government intervention in the economy, and all information reached everybody. These conditions were defined as "perfect competition."

Economists use these assumptions to claim that free markets are desirable and that the amount of money people earn is directly related to their production. But most economists fail to face the implications of ideas such as those developed by Cambridge economist Joan Robinson. She proved that, in the real world, the powerful inevitably gather more than their fair share of the rewards and wealth, and that free markets necessarily create inequality. Advocates of free markets continue to ignore this awkward reality. Markets may indeed be a better mechanism for making many choices than government control. But markets do not guarantee social cohesion, cultural strength, or long-run ecological viability. Indeed, in today's conditions, massive social injustice and environmental disaster are inevitable if everything is left to market forces. And these threats worsen as power is concentrated into fewer and fewer hands.

A second theoretical model with which we worked when we were students at Cambridge was the one developed by John Maynard Keynes. Keynes had shown conclusively that demand could fall below, and stay under, the available supply. When one looks more closely at his ideas, however, a whole new set of issues emerges. He, too, developed his theory within an extraordinarily restrictive set of assumptions — that there would be no changes in the quantity or quality of the labor force, no change in the quantity or quality of machines, and no change in technology. The situation which would emerge if these conditions were, in fact, changing rapidly was never explored by him.

Obviously neither the neoclassical nor the Keynesian set of assumptions reflect the real world. But there's more. Economics typically assumes that human beings operate in their narrowest self-interest — which is only true part of the time. Economics also argues that decision-making costs nothing and that different attitudes toward risk can be largely ignored.

On a more basic level, economists typically separate economic problems from social, cultural, and ecological ones, though it is obvious that economic systems can burden others — and vice versa. My professor and tutor at Cambridge, Richard Goodwin, an American and former Rhodes scholar, did his best to open my eyes to these fundamental flaws in economic theory. I fear I must have been a disappointment to him for I remained unable to see what he was showing me. It was some five years later, when I was at Harvard University, that the penny dropped.

Rapid growth

By 1945 perceptions of the main purpose of government were changing dramatically. Keynes' ideas, which had been largely ignored in the thirties, were increasingly accepted. His argument that governments should ensure that sufficient purchasing power was made available to consume all available supply, thus ensuring full employment, became a core policy throughout the developed world.

There was actually a massive irony in the attention given to Keynesian theory at the end of World War II. The concentration on achieving full employment through supporting consumption was not really needed then. People had accumulated savings during the war years and were eager to spend that money. For one of the few times in the last one hundred and fifty years, effective demand was way ahead of supply. People would purchase anything that could be produced. Britain, for example, suffered with rationing through the beginning of the fifties. People could not buy what they wanted: consumer goods remained in short supply. My wife and I were living there at the time and it is hard to remember how we made the minuscule amounts of food we could buy stretch through the week.

My wife and I left Cambridge for France in 1953. Europe was emerging from the damage of World War II, due largely to the unparalleled generosity of the United States through the Marshall Plan. North America had decided that any positive future required the recovery of Europe. It is true that part of the reason for this aid was the desire to create a barrier to the Russians. But the commitment to ensure the recovery of potential competitors was nevertheless extraordinary. We spent three and a half years in Paris, from 1953 to 1957, working with the organization created to give away this aid, which was then called the Organization for European Economic Cooperation (OEEC), and is now the Organization for Economic Cooperation and Development.

Conditions changed dramatically during my time in Paris as incomes increased and production shortages vanished. A similar shift was taking place throughout the developed world. When we arrived, we had a small, secondhand car and few others did. It was possible to drive around Paris without getting trapped in a traffic jam. By the time we left, crossing from one side of the city to another had become a nightmare. All sorts of wild schemes were being developed to end the congestion. One of the most damaging ideas was allowing automobile access to the quays along the Seine, previously an oasis of peace and quiet. And this was just the beginning of the damage done by the automobile to one of the most beautiful cities in the world.

It is almost impossible for young people to comprehend how dramatically the car has changed the world. Most multilane highways were created in my lifetime. When I was a child in the late thirties living in Northern England, we took picnics and admired the construction of the first stretch of double-tracked, double-lane highway being built in Britain! Traffic engineers are only now facing the fact that car usage almost always expands to fill available roads. New mechanisms are going to be required to balance mobility, land use, and pollution. If they are not found, automobiles will prove a disaster, rather than the contribution to freedom which was originally hoped. If the poor countries also buy into an automobile culture, as is already happening in China and Southeast Asia, ecological viability will be even more threatened.

Developments on the Internet can obviously parallel those on our roads. The potential of the "Web" is obviously extraordinary — but "traffic jams" are already developing. There is a real risk that, while the system can potentially provide knowledge cheaply and effectively, the actual results will be far different. The efficiency of access will increasingly depend on levels of wealth and income.

My first job in Paris was in the European Productivity Agency, a division of the OEEC. One of the questions I kept asking was why it made sense to increase the efficiency of rural post offices at the cost of eliminating jobs and thus losing a whole range of critical community functions beyond the delivery of the mail. I am still asking similar questions. If machines can carry out tasks which human beings detest, then using them makes sense. If, on the other hand, machines reduce the quality of life, damage the environment, or deprive people of work they want to do, what is the justification for our obsessive concentration on increasing labor productivity? At present we put economic efficiency above everything else. Is this a priority we really want?

To return to my own experience: my work in Paris and my wife's studies at the Sorbonne, where she was the first person with an English mother tongue to be asked to teach French, could have given us safe careers for life. So our friends and colleagues were startled when we decided, from their perspective, to "throw it all away" and to leave for the United States. We wanted to experience North America. We intended to stay for one year and to return to Europe: nearly forty years later we are still here.

What we found when we arrived in New York by ship and took the train to Boston, where we were going to spend a year at Harvard University, was an unbelievable shock to British sensibilities. The rail tracks bordered on slums which astonished us. When we arrived in Boston, we were immediately driven around the affluent suburbs: the visible wealth shocked us as much as the levels of poverty had. Our amazement grew when we looked for housing, finding that many of the places available were totally unsuitable for human habitation, despite the fact that they were being recommended by services associated with the university. Class was, and is, the hidden issue in the United States; real poverty and inequality are largely ignored. I sometimes fear politicians encourage tensions around race so the poor will not make common cause across racial divisions.

The economic reality

My courses at Harvard, which were meant to be at the graduate level, covered the same ground as those I had completed at Cambridge four years earlier. This seemed a total waste of time. One day, walking back to the decent apartment we had finally found, I had a sudden insight. The lessons that Richard Goodwin had tried to teach me while I was at Cambridge finally clicked.

Economists claim that their discipline is value-free and applicable to all sorts of cultures. It is argued that rich and poor countries operate according to the same dynamics. This would seem ridiculous to anybody but an economist. It is, however, an article of faith for the economics profession. It was this conclusion I suddenly saw as false, for I recognized that the way people in the Western world had been manipulated to see consumption and jobs as central to their lives was critical to Western socioeconomic structures.

One of the issues which has always interested economists is how people would react if they were able to earn more money in less time. They developed a theory called the "backward-sloping supply curve of labor." Their "obvious" assumption was that people would do less work if they could get the goods and services they wanted with less effort and would then choose more leisure. There is plenty of evidence that this form of behavior had been dominant in the rich countries in the nineteenth century and that it is still common in the poor countries.

The fact that suddenly struck me was that modern Western societies did not exhibit this behavior. Westerners typically go on working just as hard even when they get richer. They remain committed to their jobs as the way to make sense of their lives and also see increased consumption as central to their self-worth. This view remains dominant, although there is evidence that its hold is weakening in the nineties.

It thus became clear to me that the way economic systems are structured both is, and should be, subsidiary to cultural desires. A culture could organize itself to support hard work and consumption, as Western societies have done. It might also be set up to see the ending of toil as critically important. Depending on the goals and success criteria chosen, behavior would necessarily be very different.

As soon as I could, I met with the dean of my college. He told me, in effect, that if my idea was new it was not valuable and if it was valuable, it was not new. My immediate reaction was frustration. But I have since decided that his negative comments were the best introduction I could have had to the real problem of achieving social change. From this time on, my interest gradually shifted from economics to discovering how to create social change, although I did not recognize my changing commitment until years later.

My original career plan was to work on issues relevant to developing countries. A book called *Stages of Economic Growth*, written by Walt Rostow in the early sixties, changed my direction. Rostow argued that all nations inevitably had to go through the same stages of growth, which implies that the poor countries essentially had no choice but to do exactly what had been done by rich countries in the past. I believed, on the other hand, that it was necessary to find a new set of strategies which would fit emerging technological and ecological realities. For example, developing countries had to decide whether to continue relying on trains in order to transport goods, or move to trucks and cars and airplanes — or should they jump still further to computer and communications technologies? Should they, in other words, invest their limited resources in transportation or in communication?

Rostow's ideas were so influential that there was no chance for the poor nations to analyze their situations independently. The rich countries, who had the money, insisted there was only one legitimate road to "development." Although my interest was in developing countries, I realized that thinking in the developed world would have to change if my concerns about the poor nations were to be addressed. So I shifted my attention to trying to bring about this change.

A few years before the publication of Walt Rostow's book, John Kenneth Galbraith published *The Affluent Society*, which argued that the fundamental dynamics of capitalism could not be changed. Galbraith admitted that there were many problems in industrial societies but said that private affluence and public poverty would invariably continue. I replied in a book called The *Challenge of Abundance*, which argued that massive change was inevitable and that the contradictions in Western society would force new directions.

To produce and protect

The sixties provided very mixed signals about the future. On the economic front, standards of living were rising more rapidly than ever before; most people were richer, and there was a sense that it would eventually be possible to meet all needs. Consumers were euphoric; wealth was just around the corner. Unions and management worked together to push up wages and prices. The thought of limits was far from anybody's mind.

On the social front, proposals to change past patterns of injustice received growing attention. The idea of Basic Economic Security, which would provide modest resources for everybody and had been proposed in our 1964 document, *The Triple Revolution*, gained significant attention. In the United States, President Nixon proposed this idea describing it as a family assistance plan. In Canada, the idea also received considerable attention. In both countries, some pilot programs were started.

However, while debates about a federally guaranteed income were widespread, nobody had the courage to make such a radical, real break with tradition. And I think today that the time for this approach has passed; instead, there is an urgent need to move away from Big Government schemes and toward local community systems where need is assessed at a personal level and people are supported in their self-healing, using whatever approaches it is felt will be most appropriate.

As I look back at the sixties and early seventies, it is clear that there was a great deal of knowledge about what needed to be done. The willingness of people to consider radical ideas arose, paradoxically, from their certainty that the economy was in good shape, and that the existing social order was fundamentally stable. It was titillating to play with "shocking" ideas, so long as everybody knew that nothing dangerous would actually happen.

Once people recognized that there was a real threat to the industrial era, this openness began to close down. The extraordinary combination of prosperity and social justice toward which we were struggling in the sixties and early seventies progressively decayed. Old dogmas were dusted off and proclaimed as absolute truths.

Meanwhile, the industrial era was shaking itself apart.

from consumerism to making do: 1974-1996

The euphoria of the postwar years was beginning to wear thin by the early seventies. Multiple assassinations in the United States had taken their toll. The seemingly endless war with Vietnam had sapped morale, not only in the United States but also in Canada, and to some extent in Europe.

Three profound changes

There were many contributing factors to the fundamental change in mood that emerged after the mid-seventies. I'll focus on three of them here.

The oil shocks of the seventies, when prices were dramatically increased and supplies withheld, demonstrated the ability of Middle Eastern nations to disrupt the West. The higher gas prices contributed to inflation, and a significant transfer of wealth out of the rich world took place.

In addition to the economic impacts, there was an intellectual one. A book called *The Limits to Growth*, published as a report to the Club of Rome, argued that current growth patterns were unsustainable and that we would overshoot our capacity to find resources and deal with waste unless dramatic changes took place. My fear about the argument of the book, which has been realized, was that it would be seen as a prediction of inevitable directions and not as the warning it was intended to be. In other words, the outcome of existing trends would be seen as set in stone rather than open to creative change. While societies are now far more conscious of the dangers we face, we are still not moving fast enough to prevent major breakdowns because of such problems as carbon dioxide increases, global warming, and shortages of water and arable land.

A breakdown that directly affected the United States, but indirectly sapped confidence in politicians everywhere, was Watergate, the burglary that involved some of President Nixon's operatives. The scandal caused a new low in public respect, confidence, and trust in political leadership, which has continued to deepen. The consequent damage has increased as scandals involving politicians become more visible because of increasingly aggressive standards of reporting.

The seventies were a transitional decade that moved from hope to gloom, from liberalism to conservatism. By the beginning of the eighties, economic thinking was increasingly dominant, arguing that the way to raise the potential for growth was to increase the reach of free markets and free trade and to limit the role of government in all areas, including social justice. Challenges to market forces were increasingly met with the bland response that there were "no other options." Markets were presented as the only way to accommodate to change: the responsibilities of politicians and citizens were downgraded.

Extrapolative thinking

We have failed to understand the real shift in our situation. We have moved out of a world which we could pretend was static, although it never was. We have moved into a fully dynamic universe which necessarily has totally different rules. Listen to Dennis Gabor, a Nobel prizewinner for his work on holographs: "In today's world all curves are exponential. Exponential curves grow to infinity only in mathematics. In real life they either saturate gently or break down catastrophically. It is our duty as thinking people to strive toward a gentle saturation."

The salient feature of exponential curves is that they represent not only growth but an ever-increasing pace of growth. Applying Gabor's statements to our current situation provides important insights. As late as the 1960s, many writers and analysts assumed that because markets had continued to grow over a long period, this growth would continue.

For example, many wildly unrealistic estimates of future automobile sales were made in business magazines in the early

1960s that extrapolated past sales gains into the future, without recognizing the inevitable constraining factors such as, for example, families only want or can use a limited number of vehicles. I remember these predictions clearly because I used them in a report for the American Management Association in an attempt to get business people to recognize that consumption was the primary issue of the future, rather than production.

Today, we know that after people have bought as many TVs, microwaves, and computers as they want, demand is limited to the replacement level. We have still not grasped the broader reality that when overall consumption desires are increasingly met, people will often move toward other priorities. This was the point that Abraham Maslow, a great American psychologist, made when he suggested that there was a hierarchy of needs, moving upward from survival toward self-actualization.

Trends are not destiny: apparently well-developed trends often reverse. For example, Herman Kahn, an immensely influential American futurist, assumed in the seventies that Japan would grow continuously and that the United States could not recover from its apparent pattern of failure. Both assumptions have been proven wrong: Japan has been in a slump for most of the nineties while the United States is enjoying a rather long period of economic growth, at least as measured by conventional GDP statistics.

What about China, the most populated nation in the world? Currently it claims economic growth rates of ten per cent or more per year. If this rate continues China will, by extrapolation, become the number one economic power in the world within the foreseeable future. Long before this happens, however, radical constraints will begin to emerge.

China is, for example, planning to become an automobile culture. Those who think about the demands that such a decision will place on China's land availability, already stressed by a growing population, believe that such a route is infeasible. However, both internal planning, and external pressures by the world's automobile makers and oil producers, will attempt to disguise the dangers until the pattern is irreversible and the damage has been done. In the summer of 1996, the British periodical, *The Economist*, devoted a large section to challenging the role of the automobile, both in transportation and in the world culture.

The obvious extrapolation from current trends is that China's economy will indeed be larger than that of the United States in one generation. This can, of course, happen. It seems equally probable that the inherent contradictions between traditional Chinese culture and industrial necessities will lead to an unexpected future.

Another example of extrapolative thinking is around the growth of cities. Many planners believe that there will be cities of over 20 million people in many developing countries, particularly in Asia, early in the twenty-first century. These projections fail to consider that there may be inherent limiting factors as cities grow beyond a certain size. Can public health and safety be ensured in mega-cities or do the disastrous conditions in slums and favelas around the world foretell the future? Will new diseases such as AIDS emerge and join the damage done by the revival of old scourges, such as cholera, which were thought to have been conquered until recently?

Mindful of Malthus

Looking more broadly at the current picture, water and land are becoming scarce commodities in an increasing number of countries around the globe. Thomas Malthus, a clergyman writing in the early nineteenth century, argued that population could increase at a geometric rate while production would rise more slowly. Human ingenuity and falling birth rates have avoided this danger up to the present time. As ecological limits come closer, however, the possibility of Malthus' prediction coming true is ever greater. And when one factors in the dangers from changing weather patterns, the picture becomes even more bleak. Indeed, famines could develop in many parts of the world before the new millennium if weather continues to be as extreme as it has been lately, thus cutting into agricultural production. Rising food prices are an inconvenience to the rich; they may well become a life and death matter to the poor.

These larger ecological and cultural trends are largely hidden from us because of the way we are permitting economists to determine the terms of the current political debate. An editorial in the British periodical, *New Scientist*, caught the feelings engendered by the current situation: "There should be a special word for the feeling of dread caused by reading the works of macro-economists. As the pages turn, you gradually realize that you are merely the tiniest of tiny cogs in a global machine with no one at its helm, and that your culture, your life, and even your own private beliefs are products of economic forces that you cannot comprehend.

"Whatever the word for this feeling, the Organization for European Cooperation and Development's recent report on technology, productivity, and job creation certainly engenders an excess of it. The report is a no doubt excellent survey of means to 'boost productivity and growth through increased knowledge-intensive economic activities while maintaining social cohesion.'

"The sense of dread is, like the devil, in the detail. Trust turns out not to be 'trust' as we normally know it but 'an important asset for economic effectiveness' because it allows workers to accept organizational change more rapidly. Even the cosy word 'leisure' takes on a sinister tone."

Free market worship

The acceptance of economic thinking as unquestionable, and the current worship of free markets as the source of all good is, without doubt, the most extraordinary triumph of theory over reality in human history. The drive toward free markets is based on the unrealistic assumptions I have already described. In the real world, free markets need to be managed within ecological and social constraints.

The arguments for the North American Free Trade Act, the European Economic Community, and the World Trade Association were developed using economic arguments. They made, and make, sense in these terms. So long as economic issues were dominant, there could be no effective challenge. If, however, social and ecological priorities had been placed at the top of the agenda, these organizations would not have been accepted.

Now that they have been put in place, they still further increase the need to pay primary attention to economic competitiveness. Firms and countries are forced to concentrate on how to reduce costs so they can maximize exports and minimize imports, thus creating a favorable trade balance. One apparent primary requirement, if costs are to be kept down, is to reduce the size of the company's labor force. Thus the emphasis on "downsizing" and "rightsizing" through massive layoffs — which continue even when profits are high. It is a little appreciated irony that many studies show that reducing the size of the labor force is counterproductive.

The commitment to full employment taken at the end of World War II is no longer being honored in most countries of the world, as competitiveness becomes the primary commitment of governments. This leads to an obvious, and vital, question. Why, given current levels of unemployment, is it still assumed that we shall be able to provide jobs for everybody in the future? The argument advanced by most economists and politicians is that jobs have always been created sufficiently rapidly in the past and nobody has yet been able to show that conditions today are really different from those of the past.

I shall now consider this thesis more closely. The central argument is that while people have always been thrown out of work by productivity increases, new demand eventually emerges to enable those people seeking employment to find jobs. It is admitted, of course, there have been recessions and slumps in the past, but the post-World War II years are assumed to have proven that significant downturns should be preventable. The experience of the last 15 years in Europe and Canada is implicitly dismissed as an unfortunate, temporary anomaly.

However, these analysts are ignoring the possibility that the future will be profoundly different from the past. We must ask where the demand is going to come from in our radically changed conditions. Economists, as I have already pointed out, have successfully performed an extraordinary trick: they have convinced citizens and politicians that the real issue on which they should concentrate is how to continuously increase production. In actual fact, the real question since the beginning of the industrial era has been how to use all of the stuff which could be produced.

In the postwar years, demand has been increased by encouraging people to buy, through consumers going into debt and by government expenditures. Today, all of these approaches are rapidly running out of steam: consumption, because of changing personal and social priorities in the rich countries and static or declining levels of income for most people except the rich; credit, because people feel "maxed out" on their cards; and government expenditures because of the commitment to reduce deficits.

The question that needs answering is whether there are replacements for those driving forces which have so far supported demand. I am convinced that there are not. Nor should there be. This leads to a critical conclusion: if we cannot provide jobs for everybody by increasing demand, then the socioeconomic order created over the last 200 years is no longer viable. "Jobs for all" is the keystone of our current system.

The fact that the number of "jobs" is shrinking should not, however, lead to a conclusion that there is no work to be done. People everywhere are in need of companionship and care: older people, younger people, the sick and the dying, all need far more support. Our cities are crumbling and could be renovated. The issue is not whether work is available. It is whether "jobs" provide a context in which twenty-first century activities can be most successfully accomplished.

Right livelihood

As we think about how to work, we need a sense of historical perspective. Slavery, bondservice, and serfdom were once the most common forms of master-worker relationships. In the United States, the Civil War was the watershed that changed these patterns forever. The primary acceptable mode after this time was the wage contract: the employer was responsible for paying a wage whenever the worker was present at the job. People had increased freedom to move upwards in the society, and also to suffer if jobs were not available.

The proposals now being made for "right livelihood" must be understood in this context. Right livelihood is the most common term used to express the desire people have to make a living in ways which satisfy themselves and respect ecological necessities. It expresses the desire to find work for which individuals are competent and where their skills contribute to something worthwhile.

The philosophy of right livelihood does not imply that all of life will be enjoyable. No form of work is pure pleasure; all activities are boring and frustrating at times. The goal, however, should be to ensure that round pegs are placed in round holes and that people learn, as they are growing up, not to expect utopia. It also implies that no group or class should be freed from doing the toil of the culture. One of our current problems is that there are too many people who simply have no idea how much unpleasant, tedious, and repetitive work is required to support their "high-level" activities, and how ineffective they would be without the effort of those they all too often disdain.

I recognize that the goal of right livelihood will appear unrealistic to many. Sceptics will doubt that people could manage this much responsibility for themselves. This cynicism about the capacity of individuals emerges from the same set of beliefs that has denied the validity of all the past movements toward greater freedom in human cultures — from the abolition of slavery to giving women the vote. But the current economic decay will only be reversed if we move beyond the industrial control models which now suppress imagination and enthusiasm. The real scarcity of the twenty-first century will be the ability to command attention. The competition will be for access to situations which enable new ideas and concepts to be seen and heard. Those who are able to gain and keep the access they need will see this as a higher reward than money.

The relationship between work, income, and prestige has already changed dramatically and will continue to alter as we move toward the twenty-first century. Industrial era systems wrapped these three aspects of life into a single package. People's jobs determined not only their income but also their status, as well as their ability to experience work satisfaction.

Finding a new system

Recognizing that people can find meaningful work in the future, even though it may be structured profoundly differently, makes it easier to face the need for change in job strategies now. The first reason for abandoning the current system is that it may fall into a severe economic slump at any time. John Maynard Keynes proved that demand could fall below supply and stay there. We risk falling into a worldwide recession because of our inability to maintain well-paid jobs around the world. In addition, current levels of inequality tend to reduce demand because the rich save more than the poor, and the level of effective demand can fall so far below the level of supply that the system collapses.

How close is this danger? I do not know and I do not believe anybody else does. Ignoring the possibility is, however, irresponsible, because social safety nets are now being removed, which reduces consumer demand by the poor who are most certain to spend their incomes. The reduction in government deficits and the constrained use of credit cards also cuts into spending. Economists keep on being surprised by the fact that inflation remains subdued: from my perspective it is an inevitable consequence of the continued downward pressure on demand and employment. Even if a slump does not develop, it seems highly probable that we shall experience overall deflation rather than inflation over coming years. This will pose a profoundly different set of economic, social, and moral issues.

The second reason for abandoning the current system is that it is morally intolerable for some people to be multibillionaires while others die from starvation. Economists have conned us into believing that we earn what we are worth. This belief has always been incorrect in a world of differential power: the rapidly increasing gap between rich and poor shows how nonsensical it is today. I am not arguing for absolute equality — I am proposing that extremes of wealth and poverty should be unacceptable. Robley George, an American writer and colleague of mine, has been working for years on a proposal for democratically setting limits for top and bottom levels of income: maybe the time is coming for this sort of strategy.

The third reason we should place social issues at the heart of our concerns is that the tensions between the rich and the poor, as well as current levels of unemployment, are leading to high levels of anger. One sees this in the growing feelings of rage from the excluded groups in the rich countries. One sees it in the drive of people in the poor countries to rise to the levels of wealth of the rich and their lack of understanding as to why this is not possible without unsustainable ecological damage. One sees it in the growing movement of illegal immigrants from the poor to the rich countries and the backlash against it. The current continuing tension in France around illegal immigrants, called the "sans-papiers," is just the tip of the iceberg.

Finally, the model we are using is not ecologically viable. This is the bullet that the rich countries have not yet been willing to bite. National and international government studies, with rare exceptions, continue to argue that economic growth and long-run ecological viability can be combined. Hence, the continued use of such oxymorons as "sustainable growth."

I recognize that there is still disagreement about the carrying capacity of the earth — carrying capacity is the term which is used to describe the maximum population and production which is possible without damaging the interests of future generations. But with some very rare exceptions, thinking people accept that we shall reach these limits at some point. Indeed, many are arguing that we have already exceeded them. Prudence suggests that we should slow growth rates of population and production as quickly as possible rather than further endanger the quality of life of our children and grandchildren.

One aspect of the ecological problem is clearly the rate of world population increase. Many poor countries are, however, now prepared to accept help from the rich to find ways to bring down birth rates. In the rich countries, the ecological problems arise from the increase in the production of goods and services and the accumulation of waste. There are far fewer signs of a real change in the commitment to maximum growth strategies. The increase in production, waste, and population all stress ecological systems.

It is the ecological issue which, from my perspective, is the clincher. One can challenge economic, moral and social perspectives, putting forward alternative pictures of reality. But I believe that the ecological issue cannot be realistically escaped. Nevertheless, many environmentalists and ecologists have been co-opted by the economic establishment. They argue that economic growth and environmental sustainability can be combined. It is certainly true that current practices can be changed so that damage is limited. But in the end the increase in production, waste, and population must be curbed if we are to live within ecological limits.

Many technologists also buy into the maximum growth model, arguing that if only we would take advantage of the potentials of technology, the growth model would continue to be viable. Their argument is certainly correct in the short run but it says nothing about the long run dilemma; at some point we shall use up all the technological fixes. Even the most optimistic agree that there are limits to increased efficiency. This means that technological measures can put off the day when growth has to end but they cannot avoid it.

We can hardly expect the poor countries to respect the constraints laid upon us by the limits to growth unless those already rich are willing to commit to using less of the world's resources and creating less waste. This has already proved the sticking point at many U.N. conferences, most dramatically, at the environmental extravaganza in Rio de Janeiro.

Once we can get beyond our resistance to change and cut back on consumption and waste, one of the great benefits of the shift to profoundly new goals will become visible. The number of lifetime hours we need to spend at our jobs will decline. There is a great deal of evidence from polls and real-life experience which shows that people want more leisure and are actually willing to trade lowered incomes for increased personal time. There will therefore inevitably be highly significant changes in the standards and success criteria one applies to one's personal life. Kurt Vonnegut, Jr., a prolific and exciting novelist, was asked his feelings about living in an increasingly computerized world. He replied:

"I work at home, and if I wanted to, I could have a computer right by my bed, and I'd never have to leave it. But I use a typewriter, and afterward I mark up the pages with a pencil. Then I call up this woman named Carol out in Woodstock and say, "Are you still doing typing?" Sure she is, and her husband is trying to track bluebirds out there and not having much luck, and so we chitchat back and forth, and I say, "Okay, I'll send you the pages." Then I go down the steps and my wife calls, "Where are you going?" "Well," I say, "I'm going to buy an envelope." And she says, "You're not a poor man. Why don't you buy a thousand envelopes? They'll deliver them, and you can put them in the closet." And I say, "Hush." So I go to the newsstand across the street where they sell magazines and lottery tickets and stationery. I have to get in line because there are people buying candy and all that sort of thing, and I talk to them. The woman behind the counter has a jewel between her eyes, and when it's my turn, I ask her if there have been any big winners lately. I get my envelope and seal it up and go to the postal convenience centre down the block at the corner of Forty-seventh Street and Second Avenue, where I'm secretly in love with the woman behind the counter. I keep absolutely poker-faced; I never let her know how I feel about her. One time I had my pocket picked in there and got to meet a cop and tell him about it. Anyway, I address the envelope to Carol in Woodstock. I stamp the envelop and mail it in a mailbox in front of the post office, and I go home. And I've had a hell of a good time."

We all need to spend some of our days "unproductively" because otherwise our lives become a vast wasteland.

Creating our future

It is only in the last half century that we have recognized that we human beings are creating our own future and that, as Gabor said, it will inevitably be surprising. The understanding that maximum economic growth is not the answer to all our difficulties is even more recent. As a result, those who step forward and recognize the extent of the probable changes almost always get into trouble.

For example, in the summer of 1996, the United Kingdom Treasury Office produced a document that suggested a possible scenario for the next 15 years. It recognized the inevitability of profound changes; it also opened up some very difficult questions that will, no doubt, have to be faced in the near future. When the material was leaked to the press, the Conservative Government disavowed it as the work of a "group of kids" rather than using the document as an opportunity to create dialogue about the tough choices which must be made. Throughout the world politicians largely ignore the winds of change which are howling around them, and instead fight over trivial issues that have little to do with the survival of their societies. There seems to be little hope that this pattern will change: statesmen are in short supply these days.

The next question therefore is how change can be brought about. It is not enough to recognize that new policies and directions are required. We must also understand that we can only seize today's opportunities on the basis of radically changed decision-making systems which employ collaborative dialogue, rather than fighting with others through economic power or military might.

reworking success

part 2

the new citizen role
in creating success

exploring common ground

I n the developed world, jobs are disappearing, the incomes of many are declining, hours of labor are lengthening, and social services are unravelling. So it's not surprising that many of us experience frustration, stress, and, frequently, rage. Our reactions become even more intense when we're told by experts that everything is actually fine. And that we're either irresponsible, neurotic, or stupid when we say that what is going on does not make sense.

People can no longer leave sociocultural, as well as economic, decisions to a few controllers, while themselves concentrating on a range of personal problems from the search for shelter to a good vacation spot. Whatever our standard of living or our habitual associations, we now need to admit that each of us must be concerned with the total situation of our society. Our prime requirement for working in this way is the development of a new set of conceptual tools.

Effective decision-making

I want at this point to concentrate on the central issue which I see as shaping our future. This is whether we can, in fact, create radical changes in the way we make decisions so we learn how to work together on the truly critical questions of our time. It is essential that we move beyond the current policy debate and come to grips with the real nature of our challenges. We can only do so as we find common ground.

When things go wrong, the easiest response is to blame others for problems as they arise. We argue that if only some other individual or group would behave differently, then everything would go smoothly. In a homogeneous society, some people are allocated a large share of the blame because of their unpopular personalities. In an ethnically, racially, or religiously mixed society, there is a tendency to put the blame on those unlike ourselves. We develop derogatory terms for groups other than our own and come to believe that there are certain pervasive negative behaviors in groups which differ from ourselves by color, race, or creed.

Moving away from this habit of blaming others for problems and failures, and recognizing instead that the systems in which we live cause most of our crises, is a very difficult step for most people. It is also an unwelcome and threatening idea for many when they first confront it. An example will illustrate how this control function works. Winston Churchill once said, "We build our buildings and then our buildings build us." Thus old-style schools, with students sitting in rows facing a teacher, essentially force a hierarchical style of teaching. They were created on the basis of the cultural belief that some people knew (teachers) and that others needed to learn (students). New school layouts are designed to support very different patterns of interaction. They assume that everybody has something to contribute to the learning process.

The ways that buildings control behavior are physically, and thus visibly, manifest. It takes more effort to recognize the ways that socioeconomic structures govern our actions. Social systems pressure their participants to play their role as it is currently defined at any given time. Those with responsible positions within organizations normally have surprisingly little freedom of action, even to introduce new ideas. One cannot therefore know whether a policy statement, upon which action is to be taken, represents the real views of those issuing it or instead expresses what they feel must be said, given the present definitions of their roles within the system.

Efforts to bring about systemic change are most effective when they move beyond seeing one person or clique as the cause of trouble. It is often the system itself, as it is presently constructed or conceptualized, which is dysfunctional. Modern psychiatric practice recognizes this phenomenon. In the past, one person was commonly seen as "the problem" and efforts were made to change their behavior. Now it is believed that the difficulties can be traced to relationships between family members or friends, and unless work is done to correct interpersonal dysfunctions, a new set of difficulties will emerge even if the existing ones are resolved. This system analysis approach is by no means perfect, but it does represent a progression beyond treating patients as the sole source of their own problems.

Altering the behavior of a single individual, or even a class of individuals, will not change the way a whole system works. The difficulty with trying to change the success criteria of systems is, of course, that there are always some people who benefit from present patterns and are loath to abandon them.

Reorganizing

Declining systems often fall into a survival mode. They fail to face the reality of their inadequate resources and continue to aim to do everything they have in the past. This inevitably means that they are less effective and that all those involved become less satisfied. A vicious feedback loop develops: less effectiveness leads to less satisfaction leads to fewer resources leads to less effectiveness. Large systems like General Motors suffer from this problem; so can small nonprofits if they fail to see what is happening to them.

The least painful time to remake an organization is when it is doing well — not when it has started to decline. When organizations are succeeding, they can afford to set aside people, time, and resources for renewal. Unfortunately, success usually blinds people to the problems which lie ahead.

In today's turbulent times, however, organizations that do not use five per cent of their resources for renewal are inevitably on the road to failure. At first, when I make this point, I am met with disbelief. But when I restructure my proposal, I get through. I point out that most people are so overloaded that they never finish what they ought to do anyway. I suggest that if they took a half-day a week (which is 10 per cent of their time) to reflect on what they ought to be doing and how to do it more effectively, they might actually get a greater percentage of their really important work done. They would be increasingly aware of what really mattered and what did not. Some major firms are beginning to move in this direction, arguing that people who are tired are rarely effective in the rapids of change.

These arguments are not new when applied at the organizational level but they are rarely extended to our societal challenges. If cultural change is to be as painless as possible, it should occur when there is a surplus to distribute. It would have been far less difficult for the developed world to change its directions during the sixties than it is today when resources are increasingly scarce. The often-heard response to this suggestion is that societies could not have been aware of emerging challenges. In fact, forward thinkers were well aware of the problems but little attention was paid to those who were thinking about the future.

A shifting of reward systems and success criteria is also, of course, far more difficult for a total culture than for individual organizations. Even if some individuals and groups are increasingly aware of the need for change, others will still want to maintain old behaviors and structures. In addition, those who support old systems are usually well-established and the systems themselves are strongly structured, while those who want new directions are seldom as well-organized or as clear about what they want done.

If effective cultural change is to develop, it will emerge from a mix of old systems which do change their priorities and new systems which start with relevant missions. Old systems will often have more resources but it will be tough to change their directions. Most new organizations will be chronically underfunded but will have greater initial flexibility.

Invisibility

We usually act as though those supporting old agendas and those advancing new ones are working from the same set of understandings. In fact, those with a new agenda are usually introducing ideas and concepts which are invisible to those who support existing structures and success criteria. The challenge for those introducing new ideas is therefore to enable others to see that the possibility of a new direction is realistic, rather than directly attempting to persuade (or coerce) those holding an old position out of their existing views.

I have found this idea of "invisibility" very difficult to grasp and explain. Many others seem to have the same difficulty. A couple of limited examples may provide an entry point. We have all had the experience of discovering a new word. After we first notice it, we find it in all sorts of places. The explanation, of course, is that the word was being used all the time; we had simply passed over it in our reading. Or suppose we become interested in local history. The streetscapes of our community then take on a new meaning and we see details and aspects of buildings we had previously ignored. In both cases the invisible (to us) suddenly becomes visible.

If people fail to notice new words or to see all of their communities, it can be no surprise that new ideas will be missed when they are first suggested. They are often literally "unthinkable" within existing understandings. Anthropologists have taught us how this process works in cultures other than our own, showing, for example, that the concept of ownership in the Western sense was incomprehensible to many Indian tribes and they had no idea what they were doing when they "sold" their land. We are only now understanding that modern societies also have blind spots.

This is the reality which lies behind the often quoted statements that new ideas are first ignored, then derided, and finally accepted. Think of the concept that each of us should be responsible for our own health. Introduced in the early seventies, it was largely ignored until the eighties. Then the medical establishment tried to prevent alternative forms of healing. Today, modern medical techniques and traditional approaches such as acupuncture are learning to coexist.

A conversation I had with Charles Brass, chairman of the Future of Work Foundation in Australia, illustrates the challenge involved in communicating new ideas. He said that whenever people questioned him about "work," it was obvious that they were thinking in terms of employment and jobs. His task was to broaden their horizons so that the word took on a different meaning, and thus helped people imagine how time would be organized in the very different world we are entering. In fact, reworking the terminology of a debate is often the best way to open it up. But this can only be done when people's minds are not closed by tension and fear.

The importance of dialogue

A dramatic example of alternative methods of changing hearts and minds can be seen in two different approaches toward abolishing slavery. The Civil War in the United States brought about the freeing of slaves, but the rage which resulted from this step still resonates throughout the American culture. Another approach was taken earlier by John Woolman who patiently, over many years, persuaded his Quaker brethren that the practice was wrong. Because the decision of each slave owner was individual and unforced, there were few second-level negative consequences.

This contrast, and many similar ones, provide the answer to those who argue that dialogue is not an appropriate response to our current situation because it cannot bring about change sufficiently rapidly. It is always possible to force the appearance of change through coercion. But the inevitable backlash, which shows up in resistance and avoidance of imposed policies, will almost always have significant destructive consequences. Dialogue does take longer. Agreement, when it is achieved through this route, is durable and permits new directions to be implemented rapidly, with general and enthusiastic support.

The critical point to remember in any dialogue process is that each person is necessarily screening what they hear through past experience. They are deciding what makes sense to them and what does not. Their screens are usually well-established and the process of shifting them is always difficult. The purpose of dialogue is to alter these screens so that everybody involved is able to broaden what they are willing to consider.

Finding a competent person who disagrees with your current screens should therefore be seen as a positive development. Listening to this person makes it easier to see previously ignored aspects of a situation. At the end of the dialogue, differences will inevitably remain but the screens of both parties will be more relevant and the possibility for collaboration greater.

Mindquakes

When our screens change, so do our perceptions of reality. When our understanding of reality shifts, so does our behavior. Each of us has experienced mindquakes — a word I coined as a parallel to earthquakes — which have altered our perceptions at one time or another in our lives. The world is now different; indeed, it is often so different that we forget that we used to see things in the old way. This phenomenon is caught in the statement, "If you thank me for teaching you something, you haven't really learned it yet."

There have also been societal mindquakes. The decision that nobody should own a human being was one of them. The recognition that women should be considered different from, rather than inferior to, men was another.

Because of today's speed of change, we need to make an extraordinary number of major decisions in a very short period of time. The private and public structures we currently use are clearly unequal to the challenge. We therefore need to involve groups with many different belief structures in dialogue which can lead to effective collaboration.

Potential negative directions

I realize this goal will appear unrealistic to many. Before moving on to examine how I believe we can achieve it, I therefore want to look briefly at what will happen if societies continue within existing governmental structures. I aim to show the dangers in our current directions because many people only shift their thinking and action if they understand that doing nothing is no longer an option.

Legislative majorities can do what they want, subject in some countries to constitutional safeguards; in other countries, such as the United Kingdom, there are no limits at all. While a government that defies the public may well lose its majority at the next election, the potential damage it can cause during a long term in office can be substantial if it misreads the real needs of the times.

One of the primary dangers that can be caused by the failure to listen by the parties in power is that groups with certain attitudes and beliefs may come to feel they have been left out of the democratic process. When this occurs, people may simply drop out of their citizenship responsibilities, believing that their actions make no difference. In more extreme cases, ethnic, racial, and religious groups may see themselves as completely excluded from participation. They may then decide to make their anger felt through violence or terrorism. Terrorism is not, of course, confined to minorities. White Anglo-Saxon males are one of the groups which feel most threatened at the current time in the United States, and to a lesser extent elsewhere. Terrorism is now being defined as a primary threat throughout the world. There is a grave danger that the measures now being contemplated to control terrorism may, in reality, enhance it by further enraging existing groups and bringing destructive new ones into being.

Terrorism is a "rational," if highly dangerous, response to marginalization. If its growth is to be avoided, we need to cut at its roots rather than attempt to deter its symptoms. Terrorism is always in the eye of the beholder: it is accepted by those who are marginalized, and its appropriateness denied by those in power. The British saw the Jews as terrorists before the state of Israel was created and gave them legitimacy; the Jews saw themselves as fighting for their rights. Terrorism can never be totally defeated because there will always be some people who are so angry that they are willing to take innocent lives to make their point. But we can remove the support they have from those who would never commit terrorist acts themselves but say they "understand" why others do and provide financial and other aid.

The most intractable controversies occur when old ethnic, racial, and religious disagreements merge with new system issues. For example, the belief of many religious groups that life starts at conception collides with the tragedies caused by overpopulation, and the result on several occasions has been the murder of those who disagree with this belief. In Canada, historical tensions between the French and the English are exacerbated by economic stresses and changing organizational structures. Those who live in Quebec are asked to decide for or against sovereignty — but national sovereignty, in its traditional sense, is rapidly losing its meaning because countries are inevitably part of a global network. The arguments now rage about how Canada can maintain its uniqueness as economic ties run north-south rather than east-west. Responses can only be found as questions are restructured to deal with twenty-first century realities.

As we open up new questions in any area, we need to be aware of how our personal, institutional, and cultural views are often unsuited to those with other histories and traditions. This was illustrated during a meeting in Vancouver about the ways in which the First Nations, who inhabited the land before Europeans arrived, could break out of the downward spiral in which they were caught. After a long and painful examination, all of us present agreed that the attempt made by outsiders to move in positive directions by dominating the decision-making process had failed. No sooner had we reached this conclusion that one of those present asked, "How then shall we prepare the First Nations for this freedom?" The idea that bureaucrats should simply get out of the way was unacceptable. But the only real hope is that self-healing from within those cultures is feasible, coupled with outside help when it is requested.

Self-healing

The idea of self-healing, rather than imposed change, is at the heart of the shift from the industrial era to the compassionate era. It assumes that all healthy organisms have the capacity to recover if abuse is stopped. It is exemplified by the really central clash between medical methods which are intrusive and aggressive and health strategies which assume that human beings need to encourage natural systems both to heal themselves and to keep themselves healthy. Like all dichotomies, both extremes are wrong. There are times when it is essential to intervene; there are others when it is best to leave individuals, families, communities, and organizations to heal themselves. Today, the only certainty is that the balance is too far toward aggressive intervention.

Unfortunately, the process of self-healing raises tough challenges. When one deals aggressively with symptoms, health may improve in the short run but worsen in the long. If we tackle the underlying causes, there will be unpleasant consequences before improvement occurs. The difficulties of dealing with addiction are one example of this reality, which does not apply only at the personal, but also at the system, level. Decision-makers who tackle today's real challenges therefore need time before the results of their initiatives are evaluated. In today's super-critical world, this luxury is rarely available. It is hardly surprising therefore, that most leaders deal with the trivial.

We can only make the tough choices if we involve the best leadership we can find, who will then join together to enable new thinking to take place. I'm describing with extreme brevity some potentially relevant groups from which such leadership may emerge. My descriptions can easily be challenged. I am aiming only to remind us of a few salient facts; I am not trying to describe the full potential of each group, nor have I aimed to list every relevant one. I hope you will listen to the "music" behind my thinking rather than to the individual words.

None of the following groups has the knowledge or wisdom to resolve the crises that societies face by themselves. Indeed, if they were in sole charge of our destiny, each of them would probably worsen problems. Together, however, they may be able to find a way forward.

RELIGIOUS AND SPIRITUAL THINKERS   These groups remind us that life is not to be evaluated solely on the material level. They insist that we must follow certain standards if societies are to achieve any decent quality of life. One short list of some necessary virtues consists of honesty, responsibility, humility, love, and a respect for mystery. These groups aim to force us to look beyond the certainties of nineteenth century science and the material world on which we have concentrated in the twentieth; they want us to look at a world without certainties. One of the most surprising aspects of our time is the convergence of the perennial wisdom which lies behind all religions and the new sciences of chaos and complexity.

There is continuing controversy about whether values should anchor us in the past or provide a compass which enables us to discover behaviors suitable for the future. Fundamentalists, in particular, tend to assume that challenges to past standards are inappropriate. But if religious groups try to maintain old standards after conditions have changed, they make the development of new positive directions more difficult. All too often, their inflexibility has the tragic result of undercutting their own commitment to values, as well as that of the larger society.

BUSINESS MANAGEMENT   Management has pioneered in developing an understanding of the need for new ways of organizing work. Many companies have recognized that it is essential for everybody to have access to relevant information. They are providing evidence that trusting people is an effective management tool which now needs to be adopted in government and academia.

Unfortunately, management has not yet come to grips with the need to re-examine maximum-growth orthodoxies. Companies are also increasingly committed to maximizing profits, even though this means reducing the labor force. The idea that workers should do well when companies prosper is increasingly being abandoned, as is the idea that the gap between the wages of workers and salaries of management should be kept down to a reasonable multiple.

LABOR UNIONS   Labor unions have been one of the primary forces which have struggled toward social justice. In the full employment economy of the 40 years after World War II, their efforts, coupled with progressive legislation, ensured that growing wealth was widely shared. Unfortunately, labor unions have not fully faced up to the dramatic changes in conditions which ensure that they can only be effective if they change their strategies fundamentally.

Unions are still aiming to increase wages when their goals could be better achieved by recognizing the necessity of a reduction in working hours and a change in the way the life cycle is structured. They are often still relying on strikes, which are increasingly unpopular with the general public because of their coercive nature, rather than on educational programs.

GOVERNMENT   Those who work in government aim to serve citizens. Unfortunately, the systems in which they work, and the legislation which they must enforce, do not meet the needs of our times. It is very difficult to create collaborative decision-making with parliamentary or congressional structures. A recent news report in England showed that the children of politicians no longer saw this career as a positive challenge and were choosing other directions.

In addition, today's governments still primarily use coercion to affect patterns of behavior rather than encouraging individual responsibility. Governments also spend too much time dealing with problem cases, rather than assisting those who are working to keep communities running successfully.

SOCIAL JUSTICE ADVOCATES   People who struggle to maintain social cohesion by working toward social justice have always had an uphill battle because reforms such as the abolition of child labor or the creation of the eight-hour work day are always fought on the grounds that they will be ruinous to the established order. Today, this group seems more besieged than ever.

The basic reason for the loss of energy in social justice circles is that many people with this orientation are unwilling to recognize the need to abandon sixties' and seventies' tactics and strategies which have proved ineffective. The need for measures to ensure social cohesion is in reality more urgent than ever; the approaches that will be effective have yet to be invented. Polls show that people still believe in social justice, but they no longer believe in the way we are aiming to achieve it.

THE ARTISTIC COMMUNITY   The arts community has always been in a state of tension with the mainstream, holding up a mirror to our foibles and enabling us to see what needs changing by depicting alternative visions of reality and the future. It is often easier to see an alternative vision of reality through the arts than through intellectual argument. Unfortunately, it is the safe and the tested that most often gets public and private support. The challenging and experimental have a much harder time finding resources. As a result, many artists have been co-opted to support the norms of the dying industrial era.

WOMEN'S MOVEMENT   The growing challenge to male organizational forms is one of the most welcome developments of the last quarter century. It is leading to a quiet revolution as new management and relationship styles develop. There can be no doubt that the values which have been ascribed to women in industrialized countries are more relevant to a new vision of societal relations than those which are ascribed to men.

Unfortunately, much of the women's movement has been co-opted by those who believed that its primary goal should be to provide women with a fair share of industrial-era advantages. In those cases where the movement has adopted this goal, it has ceased to be transformative and became part of a struggle for comparative advantage, rather than a catalyst for fundamental change.

ECOLOGISTS   The primary challenge to maximum growth strategies has come from the ecological movement, which is now supported by high percentages of citizens around the world. But the clash between economic growth and ecological principles means that the ecologists' challenge will fail unless profound changes are made to socioeconomic systems. Jobs will necessarily take priority over ecological balance until alternative economic structures are put in place.

Many environmentalists and ecologists have accepted the idea that it is possible for maximum growth strategies to continue. From my perspective, this concession makes their work irrelevant, for one primary issue of our time is to understand fully that maximum economic growth strategies are now infeasible.

TECHNOLOGISTS   As knowledge increases, we are discovering that material production is possible using fewer materials and creating far less waste. This happy understanding permits us to do more with less and thus increases the effective carrying capacity of the earth. Many of those most concerned about carrying capacity issues underestimate just how much technology can do. Unfortunately, many technologists seem to believe that there are no limits to the increase in technological efficiency. They thus make it difficult to discuss what long-run levels of production and population are feasible for the future.

I would like to emphasize, finally, that social structures are under increasing stress today because of rapid rates of technological change. It is time we recognized the dangers which could result from a breakdown in cultural systems. We need to draw a parallel between societal damage and the risks which emerge as ecological systems are overloaded and threaten to collapse. Social systems can also fail for the same reason.

It is this reality that will force business to be increasingly involved with the support of societal structures. The view of the Chicago School of Economics, that the business of business is business, does not hold up given today's realities. Business requires certain basic predictable systems and structures if it is to be able to function at all. In current circumstances, there is clearly a risk that the preconditions for successful operation can be destroyed as social cohesion declines. The dangers ahead are visible in Russia and many developing countries where businessmen have to be guarded against kidnap and murder. The more threatening trend, however, may emerge from the growing anger which is now developing against the corporate sector.

A kaleidoscope provides a useful analogy which can help us to grasp the need for maintaining the underlying self-healing structures. Providing the internal mechanism remains intact, each time the kaleidoscope is turned a new and beautiful pattern emerges. If the mechanism breaks, all that remains are a few pieces of colored glass. So long as societies are healthy, positive patterns can be expected to emerge after changes take place. If societies lose their adaptive capability, then progressive breakdowns are inevitable. Today's crises require that all groups commit to adapting old self-healing structures and creating new ones.

creating positive change

I t is now in our self-interest to work together to preserve and enhance our quality of life. The primary challenge that confronts us is to discover the skills we need to think and act collaboratively. This is the arena where such writers as Charles Handy and Peter Senge, who deal with organizational development from, respectively, American and British points of view, have enabled us to see how to develop learning organizations. We need to extend the scope of our work so that learning societies can come into existence.

Polar opposites

Societies have always been focused on the past: we have driven looking in the rear-view mirror, as Marshall McLuhan put it. We now have to learn to look ahead, to be drawn into the future by positive images and visions which are created through vibrant dialogue.

One first step we must take is to move beyond our tendency to adopt polar positions, which we then treat as non-negotiable. Balancing extreme views is difficult. Charles Johnston, a psychologist and writer, has an exercise he carries out with groups. He asks people to state their views about a particular issue and to discuss these views with others who agree with them. Then he asks them to adopt the opposite view. Those engaged in the exercise soon discover that they are able to support the alternative without too much difficulty.

Johnston then challenges people to act as though both sides are partially right. This creates high levels of tension. We seem to be able to live in a world of blacks and whites, and can shift from one extreme to another fairly easily, but managing a spectrum of greys provides more of a challenge. For example, there is little acceptance of the view that both those who oppose welfare and those who support it have valid points to make. It is nearly always possible to cite facts, data, and statistics that support the positions of all parties. Those who support welfare show that there are many who cannot survive without it. Those who find it a waste of money present evidence which shows that recipients rip off the system. We must move beyond facts and data to the systems of thought which constrain our understanding if anything substantial is to be learned and new insights developed. Stories are often good ways to focus our attention: we need to listen carefully to them for their resonance rather than reject them as "anecdotal" evidence.

A second challenge is even more difficult. It is natural for each individual, group, and culture to see its ideas as superior, but moving out of our current dead-ends will only be possible if we can find common ground between different positions. Common ground is often confused with compromise. Compromise, choosing a solution within current thinking, assumes that people's initial positions represent their true best interests. If this is the case, all one can do is search for a position which seems least bad to all parties and which each will reluctantly accept.

Common ground strategies, on the other hand, require that people with conflicting ideas or opinions on a certain matter think together and learn to define a problem in wholly different terms. Everybody may then feel they have won. South Africa is a classic example of how problems can be reframed through common ground activities. The largely unknown story behind the fundamental and unexpected change which took place is the patient work done by people who enabled conversations and dialogue to take place. This broke what appeared to be a permanent log jam. Many people, including myself, were in despair about the possibility of breaking through the decades of hatred and violence. And yet, in a few short years, the situation shifted dramatically. This does not mean, of course, that nothing can go wrong in the future. There are deep levels of past polarization to be overcome, but positive movement has taken place.

In order to understand the potential of common-ground strategies, we have to move beyond the concept of "mapping" reality, as if we can know all the variables in any situation and it's just a matter of setting up the proper sequence for dealing with them. It is more realistic to think about an impressionistic painting, which is partial and incomplete and where patterns shift as one looks at it. People inevitably interpret pictures in very different ways: maps assume a clear and fixed reality. The ideas I am expressing are more painting than map. As we begin to think about opportunities, our thoughts and discussions necessarily become fuzzier as new and different perspectives come into view.

Winners and losers

People look at the world in three primary ways: win-lose, lose-lose, and win-win. Our current win-lose, zero-sum patterns of thinking are inherited from the past. We are convinced that if somebody wins, somebody else inevitably loses. Politics is the classic model: in an election, there is a clear winner and loser, even if the margin of victory is only one vote. If these victories are then taken as an excuse to run roughshod over those who have lost, it becomes easy to drift into lose-lose dynamics.

This creates a world where people assume that all interactions will inevitably be destructive. It is a world where hope is lost, where neighbors are assumed to be wolves, where the decencies of life are unattainable. The breakup of the former Yugoslavia has given us a preview of this lose-lose world. Its terrors can spread and indeed already exist in many other parts of the globe: Cambodia, Burundi, Peru. Millions of refugees from war-torn countries across the world have little hope of ever returning home. Evidence of racism is apparent worldwide. Children in many poor countries live, and are killed, in the streets. And in the inner cities of the United States, children are surrounded by guns and violence.

The alternative to drifting into a lose-lose world is to imagine and create a win-win universe. How could societies be set up so that the desire of most human beings to develop themselves and to help others develop could be realized? What would it take to guide change in positive directions?

A better way

The approaches I'll suggest are similar to many ancient and modern authorities, specifically Chinese and Indian approaches. They can certainly be usefully compared to the proposals of those who are skilled in increasing the effectiveness of organizations. The key aspect of my model is that there are several sequential steps which need to be taken; skipping any one of them will make achieving change far more difficult. The steps are:

(a) defining commitments and desired directions (core creativity),
(b) discovering the realities which determine what can, and cannot, be done (hopeful realism),
(c) finding the individuals and groups which will join together in effective thought and action (creating coalitions),
(d) determining appropriate steps which create movement in desired directions (committed action).

Failure is more probable if any of the steps is missed or if one becomes a fixation. For example, I often see an action step introduced at the beginning of a scholastic year. Typically, it is imposed from the top and there is therefore no buy-in from those who must make it work. At the end of the school year, this step is abandoned and a new panacea introduced. Others find that most time is taken by attempts to build coalitions which never move on to action steps: many universities concentrate on research and never connect it to the real world. And many individuals and groups spend all their time defining what they believe they should be about without actually doing anything at all.

When one analyzes conversations around the theme of change, one of the primary difficulties is that different people and groups see various parts of the change sequence as most important. Some feel that there has been too much talk and immediate action is required. Some believe that nothing can be done until the mission of the organization is clearer. Some argue that until a shared picture of reality has been achieved, no effective action can be taken. And some are worried by the failure of people from various parts of the organization to come together in shared commitment. Each person, as they talk, reflects their personal sense of priorities: conversations are consequently fragmented. One priority, therefore, is to learn how to stick to one topic at a time and thus create coherence in the dialogue.

While all the steps I list need to be taken, and coordination between them is essential, the primary players in each stage will almost certainly be different. Some people like reflection, others like research; some are skilled in finding allies and others like the hurly-burly of action. Enabling people to work in ways which satisfy them is a primary skill of a servant leader.

Core creativity

The dominant scientific paradigm which underlies industrial-era dynamics is based on a belief in objective truth possessed by experts: students therefore are taught "truths" which are not to be questioned. Social structures are also well defined with heavy penalties for deviance: there are set rules for men and women, the young and the old, the leaders and the led, for the intellectually smart and the dumb.

The opportunity to create personally a definition of oneself and one's role has opened up dramatically in the twentieth century. It is no longer reasonable to assume that black people, or Spanish-speaking people, or women, or men, or young people, or old people should be defined by their appearance, rather than their self-image. People are increasingly committed to making up their own minds about where they stand.

If societies are to flourish, all of us must learn to welcome our increased potential for choice. Processes and commitments are required for the future which were not widely needed in the past when most people were securely cocooned in defined cultural norms. Individuals, groups, and organizations could then take a great deal for granted. This is no longer the case.

Today's rate of change requires that both individuals and organizations concentrate their efforts in particular areas. This statement may, at first sight, sound like past calls to specialize. Our current needs are, however, quite different. Previously we learned more and more about less and less. In the future, people will need to know, in a very real sense, less and less about more and more. The basic required skills will be to understand patterns quickly and to make sense of their meaning in specific times and places, rather than to solve problems within previously understood approaches.

The aim is to set inspiring and worthwhile goals: to develop directions which will make a difference. The feasibility of the goals is not yet the issue — it is their desirability which should be our concern at this point.

Hopeful realism

Successful change requires us to be aware of the realities around us, for it is only as we work within actual situations that we can be effective. Even when we get to the point where there is agreement on the facts, there will still be clashes because of differing concerns and priorities. An article in the British periodical, *New Scientist*, written in the spring of 1996 by David Peckham about the question of whether oil rigs, specifically the Brent Spar from the North Sea, should be sunk in the ocean illustrates the dilemma.

"In the dispute between Shell and Greenpeace over the sinking of the Brent Spar, the clash was not between rationality and prejudice, but between different rationalities. Both sides were well-briefed as to the available scientific evidence, and both argued on the basis of that evidence. But there was more to this issue than just plain science. According to the economist Milton Friedman, the limit of a company's responsibility is to maximize its stockholder's profits. Shell's decision was consistent with market values in that it went for the cheap option of sinking the Spar.

"Greenpeace was bound to oppose that decision. Its own priorities were conservation, recycling, and sustainability. Greenpeace recognized that the existing high levels of pollution on the Continental Shelf were the result of waste disposal policies sanctioned by previous scientific opinion. For example, the dumping of nuclear waste into shallow waters off Alderney in the Channel Islands that took place between 1950 and 1963 would never be allowed today. And Greenpeace was alarmed at the precedent that sinking a redundant oil installation would set.

"The Brent Spar case is an example of a fundamentally scientific issue that could not be resolved solely on the basis of scientific or economic criteria."

This clash of opinion illustrates one facet of the breakdown in our decision-making process. Citizens need the clearest possible statement of the real situation, as agreed by those engaged in the debate, so they can make value choices. This means that new techniques must be developed to set out questions in ways that are relevant and understandable. The word "questions" should be stressed: the need here is not to determine the right answers, but rather to provide a context in which citizens can make decisions.

Finding ways to bring together diverse groups of competent individuals who then collaborate to define questions for the general public is one of our most urgent challenges. We know how to create governmental commissions to produce answers; recognizing that the real challenge is defining the relevant questions represents a major departure. Finding the appropriate auspices for such an approach is a major challenge. What organizations will be interested in setting out questions rather than pushing for the adoption of their pet approaches?

It is probable that most groups doing this work would report first in a print format. However, there will also be a need for other media: audio, video, CD-ROMs, et cetera. Ideas will also need to be translated between levels of competence: it should be possible for grade-school children to understand important issues such as hunger and prejudice as well as more sophisticated thinkers.

Learning will often be best achieved on an experiential basis. Here are two examples that seem particularly compelling to me. Teachers declare that all children with blue eyes are to be shunned, and they enforce this decision for a week. The experience, if carefully carried though and fully debriefed, will help inoculate young people against prejudice in a way no lecture or reading ever can. Some see this approach as traumatic but if it can reduce the unthinking cruelty which often occurs among children, it is well worthwhile.

The "hunger" meal also teaches hard truths. Participants draw lots which are distributed according to the way the world's population eats. A few sit down to the amount of food which is served in the rich countries; most have the amount of food available to the bulk of the population in Asia, Africa, and Latin America. The experience is rarely forgotten. New realities are often only grasped experientially, rather than through intellectual debate.

The task at this point is to get a better understanding of the fundamental realities of our time. Each of us needs to understand as fully as possible what is actually happening in the rapids of change. We may grasp more if we use images rather than analysis to break through our current thinking and thus create mindquakes.

Creating community

Once we have begun to grasp the substantial shift in current realities, we are ready to bring together those who may be willing to commit to changing dynamics. This task, however, is rarely clear-cut. It is often impossible to know who our allies may be on a particular issue until we test out their attitudes in conversation.

Let me use as an example two issues which have been a theme of these lectures: growing unemployment and increasing inequality. Some argue for recreating the old coalition of labor/women's right advocates/religious pressure groups which was concerned about these issues in the sixties. We shall, however, need a new and far broader coalition, if we are to be able to cope with the real challenges of the twenty-first century. Unfortunately, people and organizations are usually unwilling to do the patient, creative work which is required to build new coalitions where initial definitions of self-interest are widely divergent. All too often, groups feel that their own response is the only valid one and they should not dilute their effort.

The coalition we require in the future will be built in a new way. We shall find that there are people in all classes, races, ethnic groups and organizations who are ready to rethink while others are not. There are rich people and poor, people in corporations and labor, people in education and government. There are men and women. The patient task of finding those we need to create the compassionate era is made more difficult every time we define a particular group — such as corporations or the rich or the powerful — as being unaware of the challenges of our time.

The task of building the required overall coalitions does not happen through one large dramatic step. Rather, new and broader groupings emerge in bits and pieces. Coalitions will not agree on everything and do not need to do so. Indeed, it is possible for groups which are in radical disagreement on one or more issues to find, nevertheless, ways to work together. The trick is to admit that there are issues which cannot be resolved and to leave these aside while making common cause where this is possible.

Each of us must also accept that there is almost always a choice to be made between achieving social change and getting the credit for it. I am profoundly dismayed by what I call the Moses phenomenon. Moses, as you may remember, got to the borders of the promised land but was not permitted to enter it. I believe that many of us keep ourselves out of the emerging new world by failing to "walk our talk." We pontificate about the importance of consensus and teaming, but we often fail to act within this framework which concentrates on getting the task done, rather than on posturing and politics.

Coalition building, like all other parts of effective change processes, cannot be rushed. Indeed, the difference between what I am proposing here and the approaches we usually employ today is largely in terms of the way we use time. Insistence on birth at the wrong time is the source of much evil.

Committed action

Once a coalition has formed, it can begin to decide what action will meet its goals. There is today an extraordinary range of possibilities. The primary problem is to determine the degree to which an action will be transformative. There is an easy rule of thumb: if everybody is immediately enthusiastic about a new idea, it will almost certainly be part of the problem, rather than the solution. This same rule applies to speeches: if I get a standing ovation, I have not done my job. I have pandered to the audience, rather than challenging it with important ideas which inevitably make listeners uncomfortable. For example, there is today almost total agreement that jobs are the highest priority. Unfortunately, this goal is unrealistic. However, unless the earlier steps I have already described have been taken, it is unlikely that citizens will be ready to think about new ways of structuring work and providing resources.

The typical industrial-era reaction to any situation is to seek a quick fix, whether technical or economic. The spiral of change, which I have described above, argues for a slower process. It recognizes that one of our primary problems stems from the fact that we try to resolve problems rather than to create opportunities.

It also recognizes that there is no end to the process of positive change: it is never complete. It was once described as being similar to the task of painting a very long picket fence — no sooner have you completed one circuit than you have to start over again. Remember that there is no single master step which makes everything else happen. Rather, as Willis Harman, author of *An Incomplete Guide to the Future*, put it many years ago: change happens when a lot of people do a lot of things a little differently.

part 3

emerging successes

getting there

A s I travel around North America, I ask people what they are doing which is exciting them. I rarely fail to discover some activities which seem positive and relevant. Just recently, I was talking to people who are involved with Canadian cooperatives and credit unions. They told me they were frustrated because there was so much creative energy across the country, but they were usually unable to get people to stop and think about how to communicate their ideas. The main block, as they saw it, was the failure to understand that local community activities were important. Too many of us believe that actions must be large-scale to be worthwhile, when in fact there is plenty of evidence that the eventual synergies between small-scale shifts in thinking and action are, in fact, the building blocks toward the truly fundamental change we need.

Until quite recently it was widely assumed that the process of change tended to be take place at a steady pace. Now we are aware that discontinuous shifts can happen very rapidly. This is known to be true in such diverse fields as geology, social change, and individual change.

Discontinuous change

Why is change discontinuous? Let's start with personal change using a show business cliché. We hear that somebody is an "overnight" success. When we look at the actual case history, we discover that, almost always, the person has been honing their skills for years and that they are then "discovered." The success is not overnight for the individual, though the discovery sometimes is.

A similar process works in the case of social change. More and more people change their behaviors over time. Eventually a critical mass is reached and then there is a "sudden" evolution. Issues "break into" public awareness but the really critical effort took place long before. The real issue, therefore, is where one is willing to put one's time and effort, recognizing always that one cannot be sure what will happen and that the most important and interesting results may be ones which are totally unexpected.

What, then, is worth doing in today's rapidly changing world? As I see it, there are two primary requirements for positive activities. One is that one's actions increase the probability that ecological systems will remain viable. There are many small-scale strategies that individuals can adopt to help reduce environmental stress. All of us can change the ways we consume, the ways we produce, the ways we use technology. In the end this will lead us to understand that we are part of nature and that our survival depends on maintaining the basic ecological systems which make life possible. The other requirement is that we change our directions in ways which will enhance social cohesion. As I have already demonstrated, the impact of current economic and technical trends is to increase unemployment and inequality and to lead to breakdowns in the social order. Unless a great deal more creative thought and action is put into discovering methods which can keep everybody positively involved in their geographical, professional, and network communities, the future is bleak.

Most important among the large-scale strategies for enhancing social cohesion and the long-run support of environmental systems are those addressing the issues of curbing overpopulation and decreasing the production of consumer goods and waste in the rich world. Nobody knows the real limits of the world's carrying capacity; estimates range from human populations of less than one billion to over ten billion. There is, however, only one sensible strategy when confronted with dangers of such magnitude: we must take a conservative course which minimizes the chance of catastrophe.

Developed democracy or dictatorship

How will we achieve the necessary changes? There is a major clash in opinions on this point, although it is often papered over. At one extreme are those who believe that only a dictator can possibly implement, with the necessary speed, the dramatically new directions that are required. At the other end of the spectrum are those who are convinced that our only hope is to enhance still further our concepts of citizen involvement. They argue we must develop our practice of democracy beyond the act of voting, to which it has largely shrunk in recent years.

Those who support dictatorships are rarely straightforward about their beliefs. It is obviously not politically correct to push for top-down decision making at this time, so this point of view is advanced more subtly. It is argued that because ordinary citizens have neither the interest nor the skills, a small cadre of super-intelligent people must make the key decisions. But concentrating power in the hands of any closed elite is a recipe for trouble. Advocates of closed systems inevitably come to see reality from a single point of view and are able to exclude evidence, however strong, if it does not conform to this pattern of thinking.

There's an extraordinary example of this in the medical field. An Australian nurse, who knew nothing about polio and had to work from first principles of medicine and anatomy, developed a new way of treating the disease which avoided the crippling effects of the existing techniques. Despite continuing positive results, specialists in the field ignored the data for decades, and demonized both her and her work.

Another problem with power systems is that they inevitably prevent honesty. If you're afraid of the person with whom you are talking and working, you will be reluctant to tell them what they need to know. A powerful person may, in fact, want to do their best for others, but he or she will not be able to obtain the knowledge they need to be effective. Most subordinates will inevitably think about how the messages they send will affect their future and worry about this aspect more than about what would be good for the total system.

This is why many organizations are today moving toward

flatter systems, where power is a far less important element in the total picture. Ideally, authority based on competence and knowledge replaces power based on coercion. Despite the negative image which is commonly associated with business these days, corporations have moved furthest in this direction. They are finding that their self-interest requires employees to have the ability to make their own choices more often. This new kind of leadership is described by the words "servant leadership" and "sapiential authority."

It is now time to take what we have learned and apply it to our social structures. Citizenship can only be redefined and revived if several changes in our success criteria and reward structures are made. People must be able to make the time and commitment to get involved in decision-making. This means that we should:

(a) decrease lifetime hours spent on jobs as quickly as possible,
(b) discourage consumption rather than promote it,
(c) provide people with the opportunity to learn on a lifetime basis, and
(d) reintroduce spiritual values into our decision-making processes and use them as a compass.

Recognizing the commitment to change

If you look around your geographical communities, your communities of interest, and your professional communities, you will find exciting and creative things happening everywhere. The common factor which joins all of them is that they take responsibility, time, patience, care, and compassion. New models emerge when people believe that communities can be made better and care passionately about them.

Why are we generally so unaware of these local success stories? There are two fundamental reasons. First, today's communication patterns lead us to concentrate our attention outside our own immediate lives and communities. It is not surprising that many people have little hope that positive change is possible. We are constantly being told about war, murder, disease, and natural disasters, for only the negative is seen as news by most people in the media. It is hard to keep up our levels of hope when we are battered each day by reports of disorder and death. Typically, as soon as things improve the story is dropped — even if major positive efforts followed the tragedy.

Second, even at the local level, the media do not pay much attention to success. William Raspberry, a Pulitzer Prize-winning columnist, encourages newspapers to create a special daily slot for positive efforts — not Pollyanna news. The idea is that every reporter can look for positive stories of this type, whatever their beat. The best story appears in a regular slot on the front page. Raspberry became convinced of the importance of this crusade after several similar experiences. He went into communities where his column was published, and sat down with the newspaper editorial boards. He asked them to tell him one positive and exciting story about the community and told them that he would put it in his column, for national circulation.

The typical reaction to his idea was a blank look from everybody in the room. Most editors do not see their communities in terms of their strengths. They do not know how to ferret out the stories that show the remarkable courage and resiliency of people and groups, even under the most difficult circumstances. This is not surprising. John McKnight, a professor concerned with community dynamics who is based in Chicago, has long sought to draw our attention to the fact that we analyze communities on the basis of what is missing. He has argued that we need to think in asset terms. His work has had considerable impact.

I happened to visit Raspberry's office at *The Washington Post* one day when he was reflecting on this problem. I don't know how we got into the issue but I was probably remarking that people see problems as far more serious than they actually are because of the media messages they're bombarded with. For example, the fear of violence is far greater than is warranted by the data: one recent poll showed that some people believe there's a 50-50 chance of being a victim of violent crime in any given week. This perception is obviously paralysing. My wife and I met an extreme example while we were writing one of our books in a hotel in a small French village. Some visiting Americans spoke no French, so we interpreted for them. They wanted to know if it was safe to walk in the village. To us, the thought of crime in the placid rural countryside was ludicrous. But the images of violence and mayhem were so deeply ingrained in the mind of the American visitors that they remained dominant, despite the radically different circumstances.

The failure to appreciate positive local steps is only part of the current problem. We have also become so accustomed to the large-scale, industrial way of thinking that more personal activities seem quirky at best and irrelevant at worst. It is also difficult to get beyond the dominant belief that there is one best way to do things. Another common assumption is that there must be short cuts that prevent all the inevitable frustrations and detailed work associated with any effort to change things. There is, unfortunately, no chance of cheap grace.

I have always aimed to be involved in real efforts at change rather than just to sit at home and write about ideas. I'm constantly reminded in this way that the shifts we need do not come easily. They can be frustrated by an illness at the wrong moment, a negative mood created as a result of a bad dinner, the determination of one player to prevent something positive from happening which would benefit the reputation of another, or the inability of a complex, old system to adapt. No matter; you just keep trying.

Creating Local Change

Each useful and creative development depends on one or more people deciding they can reach their goal. They become its champion and put more time into the cause than is ever "rationally" justified and without being sure that they can make it happen. For every success story, which affects dynamics, there are many failures. The ability to create is always built on a pattern of past failures. For example, Richard McCarthy lives in my home town of New Orleans. He is passionately committed to social justice and works with the same sort of concerns that I find important. But he also recognizes the importance of developing his own neighborhood, and has therefore invested a great deal of time in creating both a community garden and a farmers' market. Farmers' markets have in turned spawned a new movement where 2,000 chefs in prestigious restaurants across the United States are linking with their own local farms to use produce which is fresher and is grown using organic methods of cultivation.

The community garden he sparked in New Orleans was developed in a fairly distressed neighborhood, providing the people there with an opportunity to regain contact with the earth and to produce vegetables and fruits which are not easily available in New Orleans or, which if available, are costly. Across North America, neighborhoods have come together around similar small-scale gardens. As the fences around the gardens provide little or no protection from vandals, it would be relatively easy for people to steal or damage the produce. But they don't. Community involvement with these projects actually inhibits theft and vandalism. Projects like this give communities the cohesion and sense of accomplishment so many are lacking today. They also give people an opportunity to put their lives back together by achieving small-scale successes.

Another example: in the riots in the Watts area of Los Angeles during the sixties, it was remarkable that schools were often burned but community colleges were not. My conclusion is that the schools were seen as "jails." The community colleges, on the other hand, "belonged" to their students, who protected them from damage. The lesson here is that people need to "own" their spaces if they are going to maintain them.

Proposals which permit people to manage their own lives can be effective in even the worst of circumstances. Public housing projects have been pulled back from the brink of disaster again and again by giving their tenants the right to make decisions about them. In some cases, this has meant that they have been given ownership. In other cases, they have achieved the right to determine what behavior is acceptable and what cannot be tolerated. Jack Kemp, the unsuccessful 1996 candidate for the vice-presidency of the United States, has been one of the champions of this approach.

Why can tenants succeed in changing dynamics when bureaucrats have been unable to do so? One reason is that bureaucrats, however caring they are, usually have their hands tied. In an impossible effort to provide a totally level playing field, we have taken away the ability to make flexible judgments which are absolutely vital in any attempt to build communities.

There are destructive behaviors which must be prohibited. There are positive behaviors which must be supported and reinforced. But the way to cope with those who find new creative solutions and deserve rewards as well as those who break the rules must be contextual rather than absolute, depending on the specifics of each situation.

Even if bureaucrats did have the ability to be creative, they never have the incentive that tenants do. Because the quality of their lives is directly involved, the motivations of tenants are necessarily stronger. It is tenants who suffer when buildings moulder and crime increases. It is tenants who benefit when they develop the commitment which permits self-policing. In one racially mixed project in San Francisco, it is the Samoans, who are often large and muscular, who have run off the drug dealers. To do it, however, they needed the support of the whole community. At other levels of income, co-ops provide the same challenge to commitment.

Where should decision-making take place? Given the power of personal involvement, why did we drift toward an increasingly bureaucratic system? There are a number of reasons. One is that communities were often unwilling to make the tough decisions which were required to prevent massive discrimination. Another was that educational and communication levels were lower in the past. Too few people therefore recognized the need for local commitment and action. This resulted in a drift in recent decades toward national decision-making. For example, the determination to end racial discrimination in the United States could only have been found in Washington. The attempt to create justice for the First Nations in Canada needed the involvement of Ottawa. The tragedy with which we are now coping is that the second and third level effects of these decisions, taken with the greatest of goodwill, are far less unambiguously positive than anybody would wish. For example, many leaders, black and white alike, fear that race relations in the United States are actually worse in many areas than they were in the sixties. It is now acceptable in many parts of the country to appeal directly to white disaffection and anger.

The mixed consequences of large-scale action has created a strong move back to local decision-making. This has been little noticed because we concentrate our attention on national dynamics and on the negative. Nevertheless, it is true that our whole culture has changed in the last few decades, with more and more people wanting their inputs to be respected and demanding an opportunity to be involved in making choices about directions. We must, however, learn to bring in everybody, rather than concentrating on a limited sector of the population, if we are to find the directions which can mobilize energy.

In the 1980s, I spent a great deal of time working in small towns in Nebraska. The common theme, heard again and again, was the willingness to put in significant effort if it would ensure a better quality of life in the community. In the early 1990s, I worked with a group of small towns in Illinois: over one per cent of the population turned out to an initial meeting designed to create an alternative future and several hundred worked on task forces for months. In Nova Scotia last summer, a major program run by Mike Gurstein — a Professor at the University College of Cape Breton — which relied on existing money, rather than new programs or grants, moved away from teaching specific skills, which were often irrelevant to the area, and moved toward empowering people so they could determine their own directions. The messages they received convinced many that the new electronic tools now available made a revival of their unique society and culture possible.

There are, of course, dangers in moving decision-making power back to the local level — for some communities will certainly fail to use it wisely — but these are less serious than those involved in perpetuating centralized bureaucratic models. We have to stop looking for ideal solutions and start accepting that the search for perfection is all too often the enemy of the positive results which can actually be achieved. There are no utopian solutions.

Self-healing

The potential for self-healing, when individuals or groups struggle with their own destiny, is inherent in all healthy systems, whether personal, institutional, or environmental. It is this potential for self-healing that industrial-era systems have generally failed to acknowledge or support. One example of this bias is modern western medicine, which often undercuts the strength of self-healing mechanisms. Standard treatments are often highly debilitating. Many doctors argue that there are no alternatives, but it is clear that other traditions are more willing to permit self-healing and that the same results can often be achieved with less trauma to the body and less cost. Fortunately, we are now moving toward a synthesis of modern and traditional approaches.

For a while, when we lived in Wickenburg, Arizona, we provided a home to an indeterminate number of cats, many of whom simply adopted us. We watched "our" cats bring home others who seemed terminally ill. We watched them grow healthy again, both physically and mentally, without anything helping them but food and love. Results like this show up at the ecological level as well. The capacity of the Great Lakes, large areas of which were once described as "dying," to come back from abuse has surprised almost everybody. The self-healing properties in the system were very strong. Fish caught in zones where levels of pollution used to make consumption impossible, are now safe to eat. The latest data on New York's Hudson River, which used to be a toxic sewer, show similar positive changes because abuse was stopped. The river can appropriately be described as being alive again.

Situations like these give us hope for the future — as long as systems do not pass what's called "the tipping point" and cannot recover. Unfortunately, such irreversible shifts do take place, for example, where tree cover decreases so dramatically that desertification become an irreversible trend or when species critical to the stability of an ecosystem are exterminated. The problem, of course, is that the exact placing of the "tipping point" is never known.

Nevertheless, self-healing is the norm rather than the exception. Once we understand this basic reality, our behavior with people, communities, and institutions changes. Systems are, in fact, only stable because of this basic reality. They must be able to cope with the unexpected and manage it. So while we do sometimes need to intervene in crises, the best we can do in many long-run situations is to get out of the way.

One block which often prevents self-healing properties from

emerging is that a "caring" industry has developed. The ability of those within it to make a living depends on their ability to impose solutions on others whether they want them or not. It will therefore often fight efforts to enable people to make their own choices. I once heard the staff of a major nonprofit organization refreshingly admit that they were, in reality, "poverty pimps;" they lived off the sufferings of the poor and would be out of business without them.

Commitment to supporting self-healing does not preclude outside help, of course. It needs to be given, however, in ways which respect the desires and goals of the individual or community being helped, rather than the priorities of the "helping" organization. One of the most effective strategies is to make small loans or grants which permit people to carry out small-scale projects in their local neighborhoods and communities. Sums of money which appear ludicrously small to granting or lending organizations can make all the difference in impoverished neighborhoods.

Enhancing Community Dynamics

My friend Margo House lives in a small community on the Upper Peninsula of Michigan. The area is largely cut off in winter and some of the money to live on during the lean times comes from local artists and handicrafts. With patience, care, and commitment, Margo has steadily increased the amount of money that the area earns each year from these activities through creating a centre which sells local handicrafts and art. The most important gains are not, however, monetary; they are in a changed sense of self-worth, not only for those who are a direct part of the activities but also for others in the community.

In her recently published book, *Getting a Life: Challenging America to Grow Up*, Leslie Dreyfous shows that this sort of activity is really very common across the country. Positive models can be found wherever we choose to look for them. We tend to ignore them because we are looking for the quick fix, the big program. These local efforts are the types of activity which George Bush, former president of the United States, honored in his "Points of Light" campaign. They are the natural and inevitable patterns when communities work. There are now a growing number of websites which set out "Best Practices" in various fields so positive models are becoming increasingly easy to access.

One way to facilitate the exchange of locally produced goods and services is to develop local currencies. If people can buy items using fewer national dollars, and more local ones, they may start to move outside the commercial nexus. Local currencies are in use in many North American cities and also around the world. This pattern radically increases the potential for connecting those who need to work and those who are willing to pay for that work by including people who earn little or nothing in a national currency.

When communities are depressed, and there is open or hidden unemployment, locally produced goods and services could be made available which others would buy if the money were there to facilitate exchange. People could then sell their goods and service for a mix of moneys, part of which would be national and part local. It is easy to see the implications of this model for shopping patterns. At the current time, people tend to shop in the larger towns because the price is lower. If, however, the actual federal dollar cost were reduced in the small community, the pattern of advantage is changed: people might then shop within their community rather than elsewhere.

There is no doubt that freely interchangeable national currencies lead to high levels of efficiency. But they also reduce the potential of local systems to run their own affairs. When a national recession hits, it affects everybody. Local currencies permit smaller-scale decision-making and therefore increase the resiliency of systems and their capacity to survive shocks.

Other steps can be taken to promote local enterprise. The first is to support existing merchants by providing better information to citizens and businesses about the types of goods and services which are available within a community. People will then be more likely to buy locally rather than from outside, keeping resources within the community and supporting its autonomy, as well as helping to reduce transportation distances and costs.

In addition, resources could be saved if the failure rate of new businesses could be reduced. The general estimate is that four out of five new businesses fail in the first five years, with consequent loss to the owners and the local economy. There is an urgent need to set up effective advice systems which would discourage people from going into business when they do not have the necessary skills and capital. Marginal entrepreneurs can be provided with the information and knowledge they need to have a better chance. Incubators, which provide more intensive support for new businesses, are also an effective tool in increasing viability.

If communities are to make more decisions for themselves, they must be able to insulate themselves to some degree from national and world dynamics. Unfortunately, the tendency in recent decades has been toward closer and closer integration. This is unsound, because the dangers which emerge from the collapse of large interlinked systems are much greater than those which result from small local breakdowns. The real issue is whether we should aim to produce structures which "cannot fail" or systems which are resilient when they do inevitably fail. Industrial-era structures have been based on the belief that human beings are bright enough to prevent breakdowns. We now know better.

Community Organization

Today everybody knows that Murphy's Law is true and that if anything can break down, it certainly will. Many people are beginning to act on this knowledge. Here's one way people are moving toward adaptive approaches, taken from Anchorage, Alaska. I was talking to some of the more thoughtful people in town prior to a speech to their mainstream club. They were griping about how they were ignored by the lower 48 states. I challenged them to change this picture by acting in new ways.

The city redeveloped an old community model on a slightly more formal basis. In many towns there used to be a table reserved in a local restaurant where the leaders talked once a week or more. Knowledge was shared and ideas were advanced. The Alaska model revived this approach. It was called the Wednesday Roundtable — because it met on Wednesdays! Anybody was welcome to come to an early morning continental breakfast and to talk about what their ideas were and what they thought might be important for the community. The group met for several years and specific action ideas have spun off and then gathered their own support. Groups were also convened in Fairbanks and Juneau. Similar models, with different names, are springing up elsewhere.

In some ways the Wednesday Roundtable is a twenty-first century service club. It's often forgotten that most of the service clubs were created in the early twentieth century to provide specific support to their communities. These groups inevitably adopted both the agendas and the social styles of the societies of their time; they typically invited people from only one sex or the other and they also tended to include people from only one class. Wednesday Roundtables are different. Anybody who wants to be a leader, using influence rather than power, is invited. People do not have to make a long-term commitment: they can miss meetings without penalties. A wide variety of topics are covered. People can be honest because they know that this is not a decision-making body and their statements will not be used to undermine their own interests. Specific ideas are spun off from the group into action nodes: the freewheeling discussion then continues in the centre.

There is, in a sense, only one rule: that there are no rules. But this does not mean that there is no commitment. The commitment is to listen to others and to learn to trust. The Wednesday Roundtable is based on a belief that a value-based culture is a necessity and that the seeds of such a value-based culture need to be planted on a small scale and at a local level. Communication between leaders in various parts of the community has been significantly improved as a result of the Wednesday Roundtable.

Small-scale Roundtables could develop in neighborhoods and interest-groups throughout many communities. Such a Roundtable might develop in the coffee shops which exist in many cities, combining food and discussion. It could be a project of a church which would see the importance of bringing together leaders and knowledge so that the community became more self-aware. It could be developed by one of the social service agencies which understood its mission as supporting interaction between existing and emerging leaders. It could be created by a city council that really wants to serve its constituents. It would be a natural mission for a community college. It could also be a freestanding club which would be formed for this specific purpose. As networks of this type matured, they would significantly affect decision-making in the community.

Effective community is dynamic and, at times, even chaotic. Much disagreement and conflict take place in functioning communities. However, order exists below the surface. People are remarkably willing to make decisions based on the overall interests of those involved. They understand that their perceptions will necessarily differ from those of others, but this does not prevent them from seeking common ground. They work to achieve their perceived self-interest, but define it in very broad terms.

Diverse and vibrant communities are like a tapestry. The colors of each of the wools is unique. Together they produce a picture. Suggesting that the colors of the wools be toned down is neither wise nor desirable. An effective community honors and enjoys the many traditions of the individuals and families within it. In return, it asks everybody to support the larger whole.

Community is, in many ways, a state of mind. It exists whenever people are committed to each other and willing to work to achieve desirable goals. It is, however, still the exception rather than the rule, because community requires people to be open and honest with each other, rather than hiding their motives and commitments.

Cultural Cohesion and Community

We moved to Scotland for the first time in many years in the mid-seventies only to find that the unique Scottish culture was dying, preserved largely in a plastic shell for the tourists. It was the old who still thought that the Gaelic and the fiddle and the bagpipes were more than outmoded relics.

The first year we were there, some leaders in Dingwall decided they would run a weekly *ceilidh*, a special form of entertainment event unique to the Gaelic cultures. The first sessions were in the cattle auction room, where the aroma and even the physical results of the sales were never far away. But this small, lonely, lost cause has helped turned the town around: we now have a Scottish music festival, a fiddle and box club, and all sorts of other festivities. The local culture is being revived for the people themselves as well as for tourists.

The same sort of revival has taken place in the Atlantic provinces of Canada, in other Celtic parts of the world, and indeed almost everywhere. There is a growing sense that nations will be more interesting if they are diverse rather than homogeneous. This movement to recover cultural traditions will create a richer world if we remember that "wealth" is not just monetary. We cannot cut off the roots of our cultural systems and expect to flourish. The real problem with maximum growth models is that only the economy is seen as critical or even important. The truth is that ordinary people are not interested in maximum growth — their real concerns are quite different. They want to be able to have a decent life and to ensure one for their children and grandchildren.

A changing life-cycle

An essay I commissioned many years ago has stayed with me. The writer described life "as preparing to work, preparing to retire, preparing to die." In the industrial era ,we were always getting ready to do something rather than getting it done. We were trying to learn how to fit within a world of strict norms and impassable barriers. Today, the norms and the barriers are vanishing: people are creating their own lifestyles and directions, and lockstep patterns are being rejected. Here are some examples from education, family life, and old age.

Tom Norton, executive director of the Association for Canadian Community Colleges, tells me that in the past most students went directly from high school to community college and then often on to universities; now the typical age for young students entering community college is twenty-six. There is also a second, older group representing those who need new skills, either because they have lost their jobs or are re-entering the labor force after parenting. This shift in the age of students represents a profound change in the way people structure their lives. Education used to be concentrated at the beginning of life, but now it can be spread over a whole lifespan.

The idea that people will have stable, full-time jobs is

increasingly neither the norm nor the goal for many young people. They have a very different set of expectations than I had when I was growing up. They often work on part-time, short-term contracts. Some find this highly stressful; others find it enjoyable.

Many people live into their seventies and beyond. Given the growing emphasis on people developing themselves throughout their lives, it seems increasingly unlikely that traditional styles of marriage will become dominant again. The purpose of marriage used to be to ensure the perpetuation of the tribe or group, the building of alliances and the securing of wealth. Most parents did not live much longer than it took to raise their children. Today, the reasons for marriage have changed. Some people will stick to each other throughout their lives and benefit from this kind of steady relationship. Others will choose to have many relationships, a style which has been called serial monogamy. Some of these people marry; others see no reason for either the church or the state to be involved in sanctioning their unions. Remaining childless will be increasingly acceptable in the future. This is the only way to get the human population explosion under control, particularly in the poor countries where as many as 70 per cent of the population are under age 25.

Retirement will also inevitably change its meaning and may vanish from our vocabulary. Retirement is, in fact, a very recent development, only starting late in the nineteenth century. At that time, only a very small number of people lived long enough to retire. Given the number of people who today live to 75, 85, and beyond, our understanding of the last years of life is inevitably going to alter dramatically. A recent evening news broadcast on NBC foreshadowed this shift: the baby boomers do not see the end of life as a time when people should be cut off from the rest of the society, as has often been the case up to now.

People today have ten, twenty, or even more years ahead of them when they leave the labor force. The period can be even greater if they are forced out or choose to leave their employment at age fifty-five or earlier. We cannot afford to lose the services of more and more competent people by assuming that there is no public role for them to play. We may not need them in the conventional labor force but there is no shortage of important work that needs doing. One obvious example is the value of bringing young and old people together, for example, as teachers' aides and coaches in schools.

Finally, our thinking about death is changing dramatically. We held a series of focus groups in the early seventies, one of which was composed of "seniors," as they were called in those days. Their top priority was that a right to die with dignity should be developed. I had been brought up to believe that it was the young who were willing to consider death and that old people would cling to life at any cost, and this demand from the focus group was a great surprise to me.

Today, a significant number of people are insisting on the right to choose when their death takes place. The question will become more visible now that the United States Supreme Court has agreed to rule on the question. Anybody who denies the dangers of this development is a fool. Of course, there will be people who are pressured into dying to save the next generation trouble, to gain control of resources and for other reasons. But from my perspective the cost of keeping people alive long after they wish to die is far worse. As always, there is no perfect answer.

This level of honesty about the impact of new policies is usually considered unwise. We are meant to accentuate the positive and to hide the negative. If we are to be able to make good policy, we can only do so by accepting that utopia is indeed impossible. We shall then strive for the best possible systems, recognizing that there will always be some problems.

We are currently warehousing in nursing homes increasing numbers of people who have no future. If they want to live, nobody has the right to end their lives. But if they feel that they are subtracting from what they have achieved in life, does anybody have the right to deny them the surcease of death? I like to think that life is the ability to grow and to help others to grow and that death occurs when this is no longer possible. This model has none of the scientific certainty of the old models based on the lack of a heart beat or a brain wave. It requires that we look at the realities of each case and the tragedies it often implies. But so long as we focus on the needs of the people who feel they are subtracting from what they have achieved in their lives, rather than on the desires of relatives or friends and, above all, the state or doctors, we cannot go too far wrong. This direction does not deny our commitment to life-giving policies; it enhances it.

Immigrants to a new time

This depth of change led Margaret Mead to say we are all immigrants to a new time. Geographical immigrants can look around and discover the ways their new culture works; indeed, many of them see it more clearly than those who have lived there all their lives. Consequently, many immigrants are able to become full members of their chosen society in a surprisingly short time. We temporal immigrants, those of us alive today, have to create new guidelines for ourselves. The older generation should not be teaching what they think they know without listening with great care to what the younger generation has to tell them about the world today. Unfortunately, our current educational systems still largely present students with a body of knowledge they are required to learn, and on which they are tested.

There are, of course, many people who are challenging the old system. For example, Jackie Japp, Yvonne Montiel, and Pete Facciola work at South Mountain College, part of the Maricopa Community College District in Arizona. For the past three years, they have taken students from the poorer, largely Hispanic, parts of town and taught them in ways that encourage them to learn for themselves rather than spoon-feeding them information. As their classes continued, Facciola, Japp, and Montiel noticed that the students were increasingly involved. Dropout rates have declined dramatically and interaction has increased. This project and other similar ones prove that students learn better in situations where they are challenged, where they are provided with the opportunity to enjoy the learning process, where their creative thought is welcomed. Unfortunately, innovations such as these do not fit easily into an academic world which normally values tidiness, measurement, and separations between disciplines.

Real breakthroughs also depend on developing links between schools, community colleges, and universities. South Mountain College is pioneering in this area as well. They have set up a system where the last two years of high school, two years at community college, and time at Arizona State University will form a seamless web and will result in a new-style teaching diploma.

I often hear people of my generation who are concerned about educational standards complain that young people have not memorized as much as the previous generation. People can, however, only cope with the inevitable overload of information by developing totally different skills than we used in the past. We should not waste our time nibbling at the margins of an education system set up to serve a vanished stable world. Instead, it would be more useful to provide learning-to-learn skills on a lifelong basis so that people can rapidly grasp the essentials of the wide variety of situations in which they will inevitably find themselves throughout their lives. Students should feel they are part of the process by which learning takes place rather than being force-fed information. The saddest image of education I know is one which describes students as little jugs into which water is poured by the teacher during the semester. At the end of the semester, the students pour the water back into the big jug, leaving no trace behind. Those who know the testing data recognize all too well that students remember little or nothing of a course that seems irrelevant to them.

Several dramatic changes are taking place in the educational world at the current time, as it is recognized that we must prepare people for a radically different world. First, there is a growing recognition that school and college must be reintegrated into the real world. This need is being met through service learning, apprenticeships, Outward Bound courses, and a huge variety of other means. The idea that education prepares one for life rather than being part of life is vanishing. Indeed, learning is increasingly integrated into all parts of life.

Second, the idea that local institutions have a "geographical monopoly" is being eroded incredibly rapidly by the development of the Internet and the World Wide Web. Distance has less and less meaning. For example, courses taught in Boston are being taken in Arizona and vice versa; courses originating in Australia can be taken anywhere in the world.

Finally, people are becoming far more interested in the skills of the individual than in the credentials they have earned. In today's fast changing world, information is of limited value for it becomes obsolete so rapidly. The people who are valued are those who know how to learn while working, who can create learning organizations which will be relevant not only for today but also for tomorrow.

Communication styles

I have talked throughout this lecture about the positive changes which are taking place in societies. In closing this lecture, I want to talk about what I think is essential if we are to break out of our cultural trance and move into the better future which beckons. I am convinced that the primary challenge is not around ideas but around style.

If we read the papers, look at magazines, or watch the television, the future is laid out before us. We know about poverty and inequality. We know about unemployment and age discrimination. We know about the dangers to the environment. The problems look so vast, however, that we find it easier to continue to live in a cultural trance. Rather than finding today's rapids of change exciting and exhilarating, we are terrified by them. We look for our leaders to find answers rather than to be involved ourselves.

I started this lecture by talking about the importance of small-scale conversations and actions. The only way that our current crises can be turned around is by each of us deciding that we will work with others to produce positive dynamics. This challenge has two parts: the first is to get beyond our inertia and to be committed; the second is to open ourselves to the ideas of others rather than continue our own narrow way of seeing. For most of us, this second challenge is the harder one. It is quite easy to find a cause and to fight for it. It is harder to engage in the quiet, patient process of finding out how people can live together in peace and joy.

One of the most exciting elements of the participatory process by which these lectures were developed was to find how many people want an outlet for their energies and a chance to meet with others who believe a better world is within their grasp. I have been confirmed in my belief that we might well see a revolutionary, positive change in attitudes in a very short period.

To achieve it, we need a new form of leadership which is committed to helping others develop themselves, rather than seeking all the credit for themselves. Lao Tzu said it best, "When the leader leads well, the people say they did it themselves."

We shall only cope with the realities of change if we recognize that lifelong learning has become a necessity and that it is achieved using radically different approaches. In order to provide a sense of how our world will change, given emerging realities, I will present in my next talk a scenario written from the vantage point of the year 2011. Of course, I can't possibly know how the world will really look fifteen years from now, but I hope the ideas I present can provide some possibilities to ponder while we prepare ourselves for the changes ahead.

future tracks

In this final talk I'd like you to imagine I'm speaking in the year 2011 and reflecting on the fifteen years which have passed since 1996. My scenario assumes that continuation of current trends will lead to major breakdowns. We need to face our current situation squarely and honestly: it is only after we have done this that we shall be ready to act in ways which will improve conditions. This is why I define myself as a hopeful realist.

As a result of my experience in presenting this type of material over the years, I expect different reactions depending on your personal views. Those who hope that current dynamics can continue will usually experience the radical changes I foresee as negative. If you are already convinced that we face immediate and highly dangerous crises, then you will see my scenario as hopeful. This latter pattern was confirmed in a recent conversation where the certainty of a major and early shift was seen as highly liberating by a quadriplegic colleague who said that the certainty of a sharp break in trend was the best possible news, as it freed her to struggle for a radically more positive world.

Scenarios are not designed to forecast the future; in today's turbulent conditions, massive surprises are inevitable. They can, however, open up thinking if their fundamental assumptions are sound. There are three critical bases for my ideas. First, that ecological limits require an immediate end to our current maximum economic growth strategies and that the consequences will inevitably alter all our socioeconomic structures, particularly our assumptions about jobs and employment. Second, the changes we need can only be made if our core future commitment is to the maintenance and development of social cohesion, rather than acceptance of a growing split between rich and poor, both within and between countries. Third, the only way we can change directions is for citizens to commit to continuing involvement in creating the future they desire.

Looking backwards from 2011

The late 1990s were a time of growing concern about the direction of the international economy. The downward pressures on wages and the upward pressures on unemployment were increasingly disturbing, while economic inequality was growing throughout the world, particularly in the United States. Everywhere you looked there was a reactionary push toward efficiency regardless of its impact on people. This approach was generally justified by the argument that companies were engaged in global competition and that surplus workers had to be laid off for the good of the whole institution, because keeping them on the job would eventually lead to bankruptcy and more suffering. The language that was used to talk about these situations was dehumanizing: a whole series of euphemisms such as downsizing or rightsizing hid the people behind unemployment statistics, rather than forcing us to face the human suffering caused by corporate and government strategies.

Just under the surface, however, new voices were emerging to propose radically different futures. Unfortunately, so many directions were being suggested that most people found themselves unable to understand what the real issues of the time were, let alone get together to produce more favorable directions. Some people were arguing for greater technological efficiency, some bemoaned the loss of a value-based culture, some argued for social justice. Others demanded that attention be paid to the environment and ecological systems. And then there were some who saw the Internet as the way to a new politics.

A new politics

By the mid-nineties, it became clear there were two

incompatible ways of perceiving the world. One of them accepted that industrial-era goals and methods were still essentially sound, that the capitalist market would eventually balance itself out naturally, and that there was no clash between maximum-growth strategies and ecological needs. The other argued that our extraordinary success had led to the point that these old approaches were making the chronic problems of unemployment, social inequality, and environmental degradation worse, and would continue to do so.

My own view was that we had no choice but to develop radically new directions and success criteria. I argued that it was impossible to have it both ways. Either the industrial era culture still worked and it was irresponsible to strive for profound change, or it was in the process of collapsing, in which case it was stupid to struggle to maintain it. I also showed that the acceptance of this absolute necessity for rapid and dramatic change required us to search for common ground. Those attempting to preserve industrial-era systems saw no need for common-ground strategies and rejected this approach. Those who saw the need for fundamental change recognized that no individual or group could be sure they were right and that conflict could lead to new understandings and synergies if everybody were willing to listen carefully to each other.

Bringing together the needed coalition for change was, of course, difficult. It was certainly true that many people had, during the last three decades of the twentieth century recognized that the status quo was not viable. Unfortunately, the resulting shifts in thinking were not broadly visible because the gatekeepers controlling the communication processes — politicians, academics, and journalists — often blocked the dissemination of emerging ideas.

However, two critical new directions were already visible by 1996. One was the recognition that the number of hours people would need to be employed over their lifetimes was declining dramatically. Instead of the lock-step, 40-hour week, 50-week year, 40-50 year work-life, highly idiosyncratic uses of time were already developing. The process was confusing, of course, because few people understood why the changes affecting them were taking place. It was also easier for most people to see the negatives, rather than the positives.

At the same time as work patterns were changing, a growing number of people were consuming less. More and more people decided that the "rat race" was simply not worthwhile. The mid-nineties therefore saw the beginning of the dialogue which has dramatically altered not only the way we think about work but also patterns of income distribution.

A new tool

The mid-nineties was also the period of exponential growth of the World Wide Web, whose successors are now commonly seen as the incarnation of Teilhard de Chardin's Noosphere, linking human beings practically and spiritually. The Internet also facilitated the organization of several kinds of face-to-face discussion. For example, people gathered in small groups to examine their reactions. Some Canadians were reminded of the old church basement and living room conversations that used to take place in the 1940s in conjunction with the CBC radio broadcasts called "Farm Forum" and "Citizens' Forum." Others took an Internet class in early 1997. Still others worked with materials developed for Lent 1997 to challenge Christians to rethink how to live in the twenty-first century.

It was also possible to send messages to a World Wide Web site which became a significant arena for the exchange of ideas with people around the world. These local and international conversations, facilitated by the Internet, were just one of the many social inventions which developed rapidly at the end of the twentieth century. It was the same kind of explosion of creativity which took place at the end of the nineteenth century. The difference, however, was that the energy was diffused rather than centralized. At the end of the nineteenth century, a small group of people worked together to develop service clubs, settlement houses, and new approaches to supporting the poor, which were widely adopted. This time, large numbers of people came up with their own ideas to develop social cohesion. Those were catalogued, using the Internet, under twin titles, "Ten Thousand Discoveries" and "Ten Thousand Stories."

New images of citizenship

The year 2000 came to symbolize the potential for a vastly enhanced understanding of citizenship. By the turn of the century it was no longer acceptable in most circles to argue that maximum rates of growth would resolve our problems. It was broadly understood that the critical questions were profoundly different from those which had dominated the twentieth century, though it was still usually assumed that most problems had to be dealt with on the national, provincial, and state level, rather than locally or globally.

It was also still thought that power was the best way to bring about change. This belief persisted despite the fact that more and more initiatives were completed by networks of servant leaders — those who sought to empower others rather than control them. The Internet had become the organizing mechanism for citizen movements; when it was used imaginatively, it proved stronger than the power of governments and corporations.

The year 2000 also saw the emergence of the second generation of the Internet. Basic levels of access were provided to all rich-country citizens, as a matter of right, just as free libraries had been established a century before. The Internet was increasingly organized as a place where it was easy for people to find material about whatever interested them most, whether in audio, video, graphics, or text. The 1996 trend toward overloads, both personal and technical, was overcome by greatly improved computer architecture and groupware which facilitated interactions and a commitment by people to manage their time better.

Rethinking inequality

Probably the main challenge at the turn of the century was to the entrepreneurs who had accumulated far more resources than the Carnegies and Rockefellers at the turn of the previous century could ever have imagined. The cry for equity, within and between countries, had become louder and louder. The arguments for economic structures which permitted unlimited accumulation of wealth and increased the polarity between the very rich and the very poor were no longer persuasive to most people.

One of the threads which affected the development of this new thinking was the argument for traditional religious Jubilee years. This was brought to broad attention through the Apostolic Letter of Pope John Paul II, released on November 14, 1994, called "As the Third Millennium Draws Near."

"We know that the jubilee was a time dedicated in a special way to God. It fell every seventh year, according to the law of Moses: this was the 'sabbatical year,' during which the earth was left fallow and slaves were set free. . . . In the sabbatical year, in addition to the freeing of slaves, the law also provided for the cancellation of all debts in accordance with precise regulations. . . . What was true for the sabbatical year was also true for the jubilee year, which fell every 50 years. In the jubilee year, however, the customs of the sabbatical year were broadened and celebrated with even greater solemnity. . . . One of the most significant consequences of the jubilee year was the general emancipation of all the dwellers on the land in need of being freed. On this occasion every Israelite regained possession of his ancestral land if he happened to have sold it or lost it by falling into slavery. . . .

"The prescriptions for the jubilee year largely remained ideals — more a hope than an actual fact. . . Justice, according to the law of Israel, consisted, above all, in the protection of the weak. . . If in his providence God had given the earth to humanity, that meant that he had given it to everyone. Therefore the riches of creation were to be considered as a common good of the whole of humanity. Those who possessed these goods as personal property were really only stewards, . . . since it was God's will that created goods which should serve everyone in a just way."

The specifics of the Jubilee year could obviously no longer be applied in 2000. But the idea that great wealth and deep poverty were unacceptable in a just society became one of the great rallying points for a changed vision adopted by a growing segment of the population. These dramatic changes in public commitments and goals altered the political landscape. Instead of having two or more political parties essentially proposing the same directions, and arguing about details, the central disagreement was between those who wanted to continue the industrial era and those who were committed to creating a changed culture.

A new belief structure

Elections in the early years of the twenty-first century were fought across this fault line. A transnational coalition, using the Internet, developed, which created an agreed global statement of the opportunities which could be seized — and the dangers which would develop if we failed to grasp them. The primary shift was from concentration on the quantity of goods to a commitment to enhancing the quality of life. The efforts of these new political movements around the world were guided by a set of generally agreed principles. Although these are now well known, I repeat fifteen of them here in the hope that you can recapture a sense of how fresh they seemed at the end of the two-century-long industrial era.

1) Stress the opportunities in a situation rather than the problems. The opportunities in situations usually have to be discovered rather than being obvious. Creative thinking is required to see what can go right, rather than wrong.

2) Encourage thinking which supports individuals and groups in moving toward more open and creative thought and activity.

3) See healthy relationships as essential to effective activity. The time put into really knowing the people with whom one works is essential to common ground work.

4) Acknowledge the importance of spirituality. We are spiritual beings: denying this reality impoverishes not only ourselves, but also those around us and our work. We need poetry and art and drama as well as intellect.

5) Recognize the importance of using values — honesty, responsibility, humility, love, faith, cooperation, and a respect for mystery — as a compass which guides our choices.

6) Move beyond dichotomized thinking. Recognize how "both/and" language, which is inclusive, rather than "either/or" language, which is exclusive, aids the process of finding colleagues.

7) Understand that while everything is connected, we must "bound" the realities we consider if we are to be able to think or act at all. This approach contrasts with the past when we tried to develop a complete, objective picture of "reality."

8) Understand that reality is born largely from the beliefs and boundaries we co-create with those around us. Although we need these boundaries and beliefs to function, we should not take them too seriously.

9) Acknowledge and empower competence based on knowledge, skills, abilities, wisdom, perspectives, and experience, rather than accepting the dominance of coercive power.

10) Be aware that strengths always carry weaknesses with them. All strengths, when overplayed, are destructive.

11) Learn that we can make progress together to the extent we control our ego needs and grow beyond them.

12) Recognize that people operate in their perceived self-interest because they have to screen reality through their own senses and the stories and myths they have learned. This does not mean that people will necessarily see their self-interest narrowly or selfishly because they will be aware, to a greater or lesser extent, of community values, nature's requirements, system feedback patterns, and the implications of "mystery."

13) Learn that different people will inevitably see the world from varied viewpoints and that reactions will therefore be highly diverse.

14) Discover that our collective intelligence, our ability to see, think, and respond together, depends largely on how consciously and creatively we use our diversity to learn from the disturbances we face, because they can show us the opportunities of our time.

15) Support the emergence of new systems which will enable us to continue to grow without damaging the ecological patterns on which we depend for survival.

Those committed to fundamental change tackled many of the taboo issues and voters rallied to them because they were tired of being fed pap. The parties recognized that all addictions

— to alcohol, smoking, and to legal and illegal drugs, and many other destructive behaviors — could only be broken as people developed a sense of personal self-esteem. Instead of concentrating on the problems caused by addictions, newly-conceived strategies aimed to support family and community structures which provided a sense of self-worth. This commitment also reduced teenage illegitimacy and the felt need of teenagers to join gangs in order to gain a sense of power and purpose.

The parties committed to fundamental change also faced up to the growing demand for a right to death as the population aged. The psychic costs of keeping people barely alive in helpless misery were recognized. The fact that no set of safeguards could prevent some people from encouraging grandparents to die had been recognized as a danger to be guarded against, but was broadly regarded as a smaller problem than the misery caused by warehousing millions of the elderly. Life was redefined as the ability to develop oneself and support others; when these conditions were no longer met, death was allowed to occur. The shift of attention away from concentration on a heartbeat and brainwave enabled a new consensus to emerge about the importance of supporting the sanctity of life and the infinite complexity of doing so in the real world.

The election of 2004

In the United States, the election of the year 2004 was the turning point. A new party, developed immediately after the depressing 1996 campaign, resolved to raise the real issues. In the year 2000, the party gained a few congressional seats and 20 per cent of the popular vote for president. This provided the launching pad which enabled it to win the 2004 election.

By 2006, the commitment to finding new cultural forms was emerging in much of the world. One primary goal which was now widely accepted aimed to limit the amount of lifetime hours people spent on the job. Declines in the percentage of people actually in the workforce at any moment were now seen as a gain rather than a loss.

The widely shared desire to enable better parenting was one of the primary drivers of this change. Social priorities and economic structures changed so those who wanted to stay home and raise their children were encouraged to do so. Two broad learnings supported this trend. People with multiple incomes began to discover that the net earnings from a second or third job, after taxes and all expenses were deducted, were often small or even negative. The choice to hold or not to hold a job became increasingly a lifestyle, rather than an economic, choice for dual-parent families. The ability to make this choice was enhanced as parents with children increasingly decided that divorce was an unacceptable option, except in extreme circumstances. Parents then felt freer to stay home because they were less fearful that they might at any moment be forced to fend for themselves.

The growing commitment to social cohesion led to a second learning. It was recognized that it was more important for children to have parents in the home than for parents to hold minimum-wage jobs. Pressures for everybody to be employed throughout their lives eased dramatically. Good parenting was seen as a contribution to society and a way to limit costs caused by delinquency and crime.

New authority structures

Today, in 2011, new ways of seeing the world are finally dominant. The most important shift is one that has become so commonplace that most people have forgotten how dramatic a change it really is. In 1996, it was popularly believed that there were absolute answers to all questions and that these answers could be found at the top of hierarchical structures: "experts" knew, "bosses" knew, "presidents" knew.

There were already, of course, all sorts of cracks in these structures. Companies were reorganizing into teams in order to become more effective; the concept of the primacy of rank was being challenged. Thinkers like Charles Johnston, author of *Necessary Wisdom*, were proposing ways to live in the tension between apparently contradictory ideas. Scientific theories were being challenged and debunked. Listen, for example, to what Richard Lewontin said in his 1990 Massey Lecture, *Biology as Ideology*:

"Despite its claims to be above society, science, like the Church before it, is a supremely social institution, reflecting and reinforcing the dominant values and views of society at each historical epoch."

Back in the nineties, most people still thought science was objective and value-free, but Lewontin's view to the contrary was gathering force. A significant group of people came to believe that it was impossible to build any theory without relying on unprovable first assumptions that could not be usefully compared or challenged. In its extreme form, this way of thinking led to total cultural relativism and the argument that there can be no valid way to judge behavior. If a particular pattern occurs in a culture, and the culture appears functional, then those supporting this model argued that nobody had the right to challenge it. For example, if slavery was accepted in a culture, then outsiders needed to accept it, rather than denounce it.

This way of thinking supported a strong intellectual thesis for several decades. "Political correctness," in all of its finally bizarre forms, held that it was inappropriate to challenge the behavior of various groups. Vigorous debate became all but impossible because people were afraid of each other. The fear was partially personal. For public figures, however, the risk was the loss of all credibility if they trespassed beyond the limits of acceptable discourse, even if they raised a valid issue or voiced an unpalatable truth.

Today the dominant style is profoundly different. People recognize that everybody will inevitably see the world differently based on their experiences, genes, sex, age, etcetera. We now recognize that there can be no absolutely correct answer when dealing with complex, open questions. Decisions today can only be effective if made on the basis of personal authority, rather than power.

This shift away from power strategies has, perhaps, been the greatest change in human history. It has only been accomplished because citizens became so angered by power games and the danger they were posing to human survival that they were moved to action. This shift away from power is the primary change that the new political movements around the world have made as they create new cultural norms. They are committed to enabling people of different views to live together, to accept that conflict remains inevitable but that it does not have to lead to violence.

Society in 2011 is therefore no utopia, but we are moving toward collaborative decision-making models which seek to navigate the rapids of change with minimum cost and pain.

How society is organized

One way to catalogue the changes which are taking place is to look at various scales of decision-making. The family is once again the core of society, but in a different way than it was in the past. Instead of defining families in terms of blood-relationship or marriage, we consider any group of people who make a commitment to love and care for each other as a family. We recognize that families are necessarily small, for it is only possible to intensively care for and support a limited number of people.

The nature of marriage is changing: people see relationships in increasingly varied ways. It had already become clear by the 1990s that many people no longer saw the need for either the church or the state to have any part in determining when and how they lived together. On the other hand, society increasingly demands high levels of commitment from those who intend to raise children. Essentially error-proof contraception at very low cost has made birth a choice rather than the accident it still was so often in the late twentieth century.

Small, geographically-based neighborhoods are now seen as the basis for much activity: they tend to range from 200 to 500 people. People in these neighborhoods are deeply committed to each other, and aim to grow and produce much of what is needed for living through local activity. Neighborhood gardens have made a comeback and two-way relationships with local farmers are also important. These neighborhoods usually support a full-service community structure. It is often based in an extended family's home and contains the complex technology required in today's world. In addition, it is a safe house and a support system for those in trouble. It also manages the exchange of goods and services within the local neighborhood and arranges for exchanges with other local groups and Internet groups, using local currencies.

These small neighborhoods of 200 to 500 people are the base of the political system. Each one elects a representative (who must live in the area) to the next level of government. The procedures in these elections vary widely, but there is one common thread: people who show any sign of wanting an office so as to exercise power are usually denied it. Instead, representatives are sought on the basis of their competence and knowledge. People are "drafted" by their peers who have observed past actions.

The next level of government typically links anywhere from ten to fifty of the smallest levels of government into a "conviviality," a new word coined to describe this institutional level. All the representatives from the smaller areas meet to consider issues where cooperation is felt to be helpful. Now that energy taxes are high enough to have significantly reduced long-distance transportation, the discussion is often around how to create the highest levels of self-sufficiency or local exchange, often using local currencies.

Communities, the next level of government, look at broader issues. While there is a presupposition that families, neighborhoods, and convivialities should make decisions for themselves, there are times when communities need to imagine and support common patterns. Communities have developed various rules for resolving inevitable conflicts but there is almost unanimous agreement that messiness cannot be avoided. The old tradition of clear-cut lines of authority is dying — though the process of death is slow and painful in many areas.

The next level of government is the bioregion, linked by shared ecological realities. Much of the early thinking on bioregions assumed that they would have clear boundaries like the political structures they replaced. As understanding has grown, we have discovered that bioregions overlap. Bioregional interests are typically represented by councils which recognize that they will flourish as they respect natural limits and suffer if they ignore them.

There have been, of course, dramatic changes in governance. Decision-making has devolved largely to the community level. Nation states have lost much power, as have their various subunits, described variously as states, provinces, or counties in different parts of the world. National sovereignty was based on the ability to control the economy and to protect one's borders.

Technological developments have made it impossible to maintain these powers. Today's structures depend less on coercion and more on shared agreement. Agreement is achieved locally through face-to-face discussions and globally through networking.

One of the most fascinating shifts in the last 15 years has been the changes in the way that national identity is understood. For example, in Great Britain, national power has largely devolved back to England, Ireland, Scotland, and Wales. The sense of shared history, without political coercion, has led to closer relationships at the personal and cultural level than ever existed in the past both within these units and between them. Canada has rediscovered that, despite its immense size and relatively sparse population, it is joined by a common sense understanding of the public good. Once it was recognized that industrial-era versions of sovereignty were essentially meaningless, many of the issues which had caused so much tension in the late twentieth century turned out to be relatively unimportant.

Community-based government

The inevitable result of the movement toward community decision-making is much greater variation in the situations within communities. Some have developed strong commitments to all the people within them as the poorer members of the society have realized their need for education and involvement. Some areas are distressingly unjust. It has been realized, with considerable pain and grief, that there is no substitute for local effort and that if people are not prepared to look after their own destiny, it cannot be taken care of by "big government."

Nevertheless, there is still a possibility of appealing to larger levels of political organization. If the power structure in a neighborhood or a community is clearly refusing to permit citizens to be involved in decision-making, then there is a process to bring in outside support. It can be triggered if 60 per cent of those in an area petition for outside intervention.

One reason the community-based approach works is that most funds for those who need help are now generated locally. There has been a dramatic decrease in national, state, and provincial tax rates associated with a decrease in their responsibilities. This has freed up resources which are now used more effectively locally. Military expenditures have also declined dramatically.

The question of the appropriate level of transfers between richer and poorer people, richer and poorer areas of countries, and between rich and poor countries worldwide is still, of course, not resolved. The pathologies of aid are today far more fully understood. On the other hand, the challenge of supporting those who cannot develop resources for themselves is being recognized. The transfers that take place are now almost always locally controlled and far more emphasis is placed on small or micro loans and grants.

Those countries, and companies, which deny or ignore shared cultural and ecological commitments find that penalties are heavy. This distresses some people who still feel that companies and countries should be able to do whatever they wish. But there is more and more general agreement that we should not countenance behavior that damages ecological systems or fails to support basic human rights. This result could have been foreseen in the mid-1990s. Companies and countries were already discovering that their well-funded public relations mechanisms could be overwhelmed by public outrage. Today, the successors to the Internet make it possible for public opinion to be organized rapidly. Those who have felt the weight of anger which can develop so rapidly have become far more cautious in their decision-making.

Work, jobs, and income

The questions of work, purpose, jobs, resources, prestige, and the relationships between them have seen some of the sharpest changes. Computers and robots have taken over a great deal of the menial, unappealing, unattractive, and dangerous toil. Given that nearly everybody in the rich world has basic economic security, although the methods chosen to achieve this goal vary widely, people can largely choose what they want to do. Today we understand that most people want to work at tasks which make sense of their lives. They do not do this work because it earns them money but because they enjoy it. The norm is now for people to work on what matters to them, rather than struggling with a job they may detest just to pay the bills.

There was massive opposition to tampering with the job system. Many feared that people would cease to work if they were not forced to do so by the need to earn their living. Others felt that the unpleasant work would not get done at all. While there are, as expected, some difficulties with both these issues, they have proven to be minor.

The emphasis on parenting, increasingly seen as important work, has continued to develop. If one parent wishes to stay home and raise children, both communities and firms are developing ways to make this possible without significant financial sacrifice. It is increasingly understood that the skills gained in parenting are directly relevant to the needed work of 2011. Parents inevitably have to know how to think for themselves and that's the most important criterion for a good worker in 2011. Parenting is being "automatically" combined with access to the public world through electronic networking.

The establishment of sabbaticals for growing numbers of workers has been one of the strongest trends in recent years. There are many ways workers can earn the right to take several months off from work in order to concentrate on learning. Sabbaticals are, of course, part of much broader changes in the life-cycle, including the effective abandonment of the concepts of adolescence and retirement.

Everybody is expected during their teenage years to give two years of community service. There are multiple benefits: the activities provide heavy physical activity at a time when young people need it; it puts people in touch with those from other religious and ethnic groups and classes whom they otherwise might not meet; and it provides a labor force for activities that people choose not to do later in life.

Tax policy has altered. Upper and lower limits have been set on retained wealth on a worldwide scale. A few areas are still failing to enact this legislation, but the trend is irreversible and the loopholes for millionaires and billionaires are becoming narrower and narrower. Taxes are designed to decrease consumption; investment is increasingly used to reduce waste and the use of nonrenewable resources.

I suppose that the main shift that somebody jumping over the 15 years since 1996 would notice is that our pace of life is far more relaxed. It is true that those engaged in certain types of activity do have to work extraordinarily hard, but we recognize that such intensive activities should be limited in time. Tired people necessarily narrow their thinking and this is unacceptable in a rapidly changing world.

What we think valuable is quite different. We believe that fun and joy are critical to life. We appreciate relationships for the richness they give to our perceptions. We have learned to enjoy our uncertain world rather than to be frustrated by it. Not knowing what lies around the corner is what keeps life worth living.

Poor country issues

I cannot end this scenario without mentioning the poor countries. This is a subject which would take its own set of talks to handle adequately. In summary, I can say that the decision of the rich countries to abandon maximum-growth models has opened up the potential for the redefinition of desirable developmental strategies which concentrate on the quality of life, rather than the quality of products.

Poverty in 2011 is still a massive problem in many parts of the world. But as birthrates drop dramatically as a result of the wider education of women and the availability of contraceptives — the Catholic Church abandoned its opposition with the new Pope — there are signs that the corner is being turned.

The experience of Kerala, one of the Indian provinces, is increasingly cited as a model. Despite its relatively low per capita income, it has extraordinarily high standards of health and education. Its life expectancies are similar to those of the rich countries. Kerala provides clear-cut evidence that social justice and social cohesion are possible without high levels of consumption.

One of the most rapidly growing movements is the commitment of the people of Kerala and other similar areas to learning how one can provide a high quality of life using far fewer resources. The flow of ideas which in the 1990s was around how to increase material consumption is now concentrated on how we can live in joy and spirituality.

your place in future thinking

I have described a positive scenario for the next 15 years, a scenario that places a high priority on social cohesion and that redefines the meaning of development and growth. There are other possible scenarios one could imagine for our future. One would link high economic growth and high social cohesion. Another would combine high economic growth and low social cohesion. And still another would couple low economic growth and low social cohesion, although it is difficult to imagine why anybody would choose this as their preferred option.

As mentioned earlier, a group of senior Canadian public servants and private-sector executives, working with researchers and international authorities, has been meeting recently under the auspices of the Parliamentary Centre and the Meridian International Institute to decide which scenarios are credible. They have concluded, as I do, that low social cohesion would be dangerous: "One striking realization that emerged for us, as we reviewed the scenarios, was that we could design a relatively desirable scenario even if we did not postulate a new economic boom. But we could not come up with a scenario in which any of us would want to live, if we did not postulate success in building social cohesion."

Any low social cohesion model was therefore found unacceptable and was excluded. Those involved in the study believed both the high-growth and low-growth models were possible. I, on the other hand, am convinced that high rates of economic growth, in the conventional sense, are infeasible because of ecological constraints, which is why my scenario stresses high social cohesion and the abandonment of maximum economic growth models.

Those of you who have followed my thinking will know that the scenario I've developed is not the one I consider most probable: our probable future is negative. If we do not change directions rapidly, the impact of technology will deprive many people of the possibility of earning a living, and this will lead to despair and disruption. In addition, rampant technology will leach the meaning out of life.

The Old Testament tells us that without vision the people perish, and other religions have similar tenets. The purpose of these lectures has been to provide chewy food for new thought — rather than predigested pap. It is certain that events will not develop in the way I describe, but I believe our chances improve , the more we talk and act together creatively.

All of us learn by having the opportunity to test our emerging ideas in safe places. There are today few places to think creatively about the opportunities our emerging world provides. One of the results of the cancellation of the Massey lectures has been to enhance the energy and dynamics which are going toward rethinking appropriate goals for the twenty-first century.

I am sometimes asked whether my almost forty years of work on the issues of fundamental change has left me discouraged. I am both despairing and profoundly hopeful — despairing if we allow current trends to continue, immensely hopeful if only the many competent and compassionate people decide to think and act together. I am sometimes asked why I continue to do this work. My answer is that I meet a better class of people, I have more fun, and I would like to see what human beings can co-create when they decide to grasp opportunities rather than mire themselves in problems.

From time to time I like to imagine an evening in the 2020s. By this time the years around the turn of the century will have taken on an heroic glow, and our children and grandchildren will ask what we did to create the better world in which we will then, I hope, be living. I would like all of us to have many stories to tell of the exciting roles we played which helped move us toward our more peaceful and joyous world.

The material in this volume is designed to teach less and less about more and more. A bibliography which covered all of the points would be as long as the book! I believe that when information doubles, knowledge halves and wisdom quarters. I have aimed to provide starting points in a number of fields. All of them will provide you with plenty of branches for further learning. Today it is all too easy to overload people and add to the "info glut." So this is a small, personal set of preferred readings.

This set of lectures is based on a belief that current dynamics will cause economic, moral, social, ecological, and spiritual crises. A recent volume by Angus Reid, *Turning Point to Shakedown* (Doubleday, Toronto), uses polling data to show some of the issues which inevitably arise if unemployment remains high. He argues that demand cannot recover in these conditions, and that the danger of a slump continues to increase, as does the threat of a breakdown in the social order. The argument by Reed, and many other writers, makes it clear that we must move toward a scenario which is based on high social cohesion and a radically changed concept of development. Such a model would require us to create a very different "game" than the one in which we are all engaged at the current time.

My approach is one variant of the style of thinking which assumes that ecological integrity, effective decision-making, and social cohesion are vital. Others place their priorities elsewhere. *Changing Maps: Governing in a World of Rapid Change*, edited by Steven A. Rosell (Carleton University Press, Ottawa), which reflects the views of a small group of Canadians from the private and public sector, provides an overview of various possible futures.

Charles Handy comes at the same set of issues from a

pragmatic, industrial-era point of view, and has written several books. The one I like best is *The Empty Raincoat: Making Sense of the Future* (Arrow Business Books). He shows that economic and social norms are already changing under us but few people are willing to face this reality. One of his primary conclusions is that lifetime hours of work will inevitably decline in the next generation and that dramatic shifts in the social contract are therefore inevitable.

Jeremy Rifkin pushes this argument further in *The End of Work: the Decline of the Global Labor Force and the Dawn of the Post-Market Era* (Putnam, New York). He develops a compelling argument about the decline in the availability of jobs; it has drawn considerable attention. The solution he proposes at the end of his book seems to me insufficiently radical: he wants to maintain jobs but have them paid for by community organizations. I, on the other hand, believe that the very concept of jobs is obsolescent and that we must move on to thinking about "right livelihood" where people do work they like.

This theme is developed by Matthew Fox in *The Reinvention of Work: a New Vision of Livelihood for Our Time* (Harper San Francisco). While these two approaches, and many others, will inevitably be meshed during the transition, there can be no doubt that the varied emphases of Fox and Rifkin will lead societies to concentrate their attention in very different directions.

Leslie Dreyfous explores, in *Getting a Life: Challenging America to Grow Up* (Gold Leaf Press, Murray, Utah), how this difference in view works out in communities. She shows that people no longer believe that governments at any level can solve their problems. They are recreating their communities by learning how to work and share together and by going back to times when more relationships were personal rather than market-driven.

In *Beyond Poverty and Affluence* (University of Toronto Press), Bob Goudzwaard and Harry De Lange examine the extent of changes which are necessary if society is to move, as their subtitle expresses it, "Towards a Canadian Economy of Care." This book, developed in Holland and now used broadly for study purposes, shows how much change is necessary if people, rather than economies, are to be the centre of attention.

I take up the same set of themes in *Turning the Century* (Participation Publishers, E 525 Mission, Spokane, WA 99202), a volume which suggests specific directions for economies, societies, and decision-making systems. This book enlarges on the themes which are sketched in this volume and makes specific proposals for change.

Lying behind the necessity for all these changes are the ecological imperatives of our time. In *Our Ecological Footprint: Reducing Human Impact on the Earth* (New Society Publishers, Gabriola Island), Mathis Wackernagel and William Rees have aimed to make the issues comprehensible by using the concept of a footprint: this describes how much land people are using to support their lifestyle. The larger the footprint, the more urgent our ecological problems become.

It is this ecological constraint, which was strongly expressed at the international conference in Rio, which is forcing new directions upon us. Unfortunately, our decision-making is not keeping up with the challenges. In *Beyond Left and Right: Breaking the Political Stalemate* (Institute for Contemporary Studies, San Francisco), A. Lawrence Chickering explores how the complexities of right/left politics get in the way of clear thinking and argues for a new pattern of thought.

Ursula Franklin takes Chickering's concerns further in *The Real World of Technology* (Anansi, Toronto), and argues that only large-scale dialogue can produce the mindquakes necessary for the speed and size of change we currently require. This theme resonates strongly with my central arguments.

Serious work on fundamental change inevitably requires one to evaluate relative "impossibilities." Rational analysis will inevitably lead to the conclusion that inertia is stronger than the forces which can be mobilized for renewal. Desmond Berghofer's *The Visioneers: A Courage Story about Belief in the Future* (Creative Learning International Press, Toronto) is a story about how the improbable happened. A number of other writers are developing convergent scenarios.

A second, more pragmatic, approach to how decision-making authority might shift is contained in *Grass-shoots*

(Participation Publishers, E 525 Mission, Spokane, WA 99202). This describes how a social movement, originally intended to strengthen communities, develops into a political strategy as current governments are unable to deal with the new type of demands which are created by committed citizens.

Finally, I want to open a broader set of horizons. There are a great many volumes which deal with the underlying shifts in the way we need to think about how the world works. One of the classics is Gregory Bateson's *Steps to an Ecology of Mind* (J.Aronson, Northvale, NJ). One of the greatest thinkers of this century, he opens up many of the issues with which we need to struggle.

Chaos: Making a New Science by James Gleick (Viking, New York) takes one part of this shift in perspective and manages to describe a totally new way of seeing the world in fully comprehensible terms. The book will enable you to put on a new set of spectacles: conventional nineteenth century physical science becomes a special case of a far broader set of phenomena.

In this new world, leadership is still necessary but its style must be profoundly different. *Servant Leadership: a Journey into the Nature of Legitimate Power and Greatness* by Robert Greenleaf (Paulist Press, New York) makes it possible to understand that top-down leadership does not work, and prevents us from falling into the alternative pathology of relying on totally flat systems. The book gives content to Lao Tzu's statement, "When the leader leads well, the people say they did it themselves."

If you want a much broader list, and you are on the Internet, you can visit our Informational Transformational Learning Centre at

transform.org/transform/tlc/index.html

This site will also enable you to order directly any of the books listed here. If you want to work interactively, join us on

http://www.skywalk.com/~caucus/

If you want to contact me, you can write to:

rtheobald@igc.apc.org

or, by snail-mail, at

E 525 Mission, Spokane, WA 99202.

The cancellation of the Massey lectures has clearly created more energy than might have been expected if they had actually been broadcast. It is my hope that what happens in this country can be sufficiently dynamic that it will serve as a model for other nations. Those who want to explore the potentials should work through the web-sites or contact me directly.

Sustainability
Community
Nonviolence
Feminism
Progressive Leadership
Educational & Parenting Resources

NEW SOCIETY PUBLISHERS
BOOKS TO BUILD A NEW SOCIETY